Living Through History

THE FRENCH REVOLUTION

ELIZABETH AND JAMES CAMPLING

Batsford Academic and Educational
London

ACKNOWLEDGMENTS

The Authors and Publishers thank the following for their kind permission to reproduce copyright illustrations: Bibliothèque Nationale, Paris, figures 45, 48, 50, 58; Mary Evans Picture Library, figures 19, 39; Mandel Archive, figures 24, 57; Mansell Collection Ltd, figures 4, 5, 6, 8, 9, 11, 13, 14, 15, 16, 17, 18, 20, 21 (Photographie Bulloz, Paris Louvre), 22, 23, 26, 27, 28, 29 (Photographie Bulloz, Musée de Carnavalet), 30, 31, 32, 33, 34, 35, 36, 37, 38, 40, 41, 42, 43, 44, 46, 47, 49, 51, 52, 53, 54, 55, 56; Photographie Bulloz, figure 10 (Paris Louvre); Photographie Giraudon, figures 2 (Paris Louvre), 3 (Château de Versailles), 12, 25 (Paris Musée de Carnavalet). The pictures were researched by Patricia Mandel. Figures 1 and 7 were drawn by R.F. Brien.

Cover photos

The colour photograph on the front cover shows The Taking of the Bastille (BBC Hulton Picture Library). The portrait of Chateaubriand and the picture of the guillotine are reproduced courtesy of the Mansell Collection Ltd.

© Elizabeth and James Campling 1984
First published 1984

All rights reserved. No part of this publication may be reproduced, in any form or by any means, without permission from the Publisher

Typeset by Tek-Art Ltd, West Wickham, Kent
Printed in Spain
for the publishers
Batsford Academic and Educational,
an imprint of B.T. Batsford Ltd,
4 Fitzhardinge Street
London W1H 0AH

ISBN 0 7134 3848 7

Contents

LIST OF ILLUSTRATIONS	4
ON THE EDGE OF THE PRECIPICE: FRANCE AND HER CRITICS, 1789	5
THE MEN WHO MADE THE REVOLUTION:	
Jean-Baptiste Humbert	11
Honoré Gabriel Riqueti, Comte de Mirabeau	13
Louis-Antoine de Saint-Just	16
Jean-Baptiste Carrier	18
Paul de Thiebault	21
Jacques-Louis David	24
Nicholas Guenot	26
THE OPPONENTS OF THE REVOLUTION:	
Madame de la Tour du Pin	29
François-René de Chateaubriand	33
Baron de Batz	35
Charlotte Corday	37
Raoul Hesdin	40
THE VICTIMS OF THE REVOLUTION:	
Louis Philippe, Duke of Orleans	43
The Renault Family	46
Adrienne de Lafayette	48
Grace Dalrymple Elliot	51
THE SURVIVORS:	
Joseph Fouché	55
André Massena and Jean-Baptiste Bernadotte	58
Cochon de Lapperant	60
BIOGRAPHICAL NOTES ON OTHER PERSONALITIES OF THE REVOLUTION	61
DATE LIST	66
THE REVOLUTIONARY CALENDAR	67
GLOSSARY	68
BOOKS FOR FURTHER READING	71
INDEX	71

The Illustrations

1	Map of France, 1793	5
2	Famille de paysans, by Le Nain	6
3	Louis XVI at Reims	6
4	Cartoon on the royal family	7
5	Opening of the Estates General	8
6	Oath of the Tennis Court	8
7	Map of Paris	9
8	Storming the Bastille	12
9	Prisoners released from the Bastille	13
10	Mirabeau	14
11	Mirabeau in Paradise	15
12	Saint-Just	16
13	"Le patriote exclusif"	17
14	The Girondins sent to prison	17
15	The guillotine at Nantes, 1793	19
16	Carrier at Nantes	19
17	The flag bearer	19
18	Enrolling for military service, July 1792	22
19	Battle of Jemappes	23
20	David (self-portrait)	25
21	Marie Antoinette on her way to the guillotine	25
22	The Festival of Reason	26
23	"The Last Roll Call of the Condemned"	27
24	Le Concert	29
25	Emigrés, 1789	30
26	Execution of Louis XVI	31
27	Chateaubriand	33
28	Carrying the heads of Flesselles and de Launay	34
29	Baron de Batz	36
30	Trial of Danton	37
31	Charlotte Corday	39
32	Marat, by David	39
33	La Philosophie Devenue Folle (cartoon)	41
34	Philippe Egalité	43
35	March of the women to Versailles	45
36	The arrest of Cecile Renault	46
37	The guillotine	47
38	Fouquier-Tinville	47
39	Lafayette	49
40	The old noblesse	50
41	Taking the Tuileries	51
42	A house-search	52
43	The tumbril to the guillotine	53
44	The trial of Fouquier-Tinville	54
45	Napoleon Bonaparte	54
46	Fouché	56
47	Lyons massacres	56
48	Massena	59
49	Bernadotte	59
50	English cartoon on the revolutionaries	61
51	Barras	61
52	Danton	62
53	Robespierre	64
54	The death of the Church (cartoon)	65
55	Le Jacobin	69
56	The Constitution, 1791	69
57	9/10 Thermidor (cartoon)	70
58	Vendéan rebel	70

ON THE EDGE OF THE PRECIPICE: FRANCE AND HER CRITICS, 1789

France in the late eighteenth century was a country in crisis. A failed foreign policy had combined with incompetent domestic administration to bring about a virtual collapse of the financial system. Thomas Jefferson, United States ambassador to France between 1784 and 1789, was highly critical of the government to which he had been accredited. Out of a population:

of twenty millions of people supposed to be in France, there are nineteen million more wretched, more accursed in every circumstance of human existence, than the most conspicuously wretched individual of the whole United States.

This state of affairs he attributed to:

kings, nobles and priests, and to them alone . . . under the pretext of governing they have divided the nation into two classes, wolves and sheep.

There were many in France who agreed with him. After all, the American revolution of 1776 itself had owed much to the writings of the French philosophers, Voltaire, Montesquieu and Rousseau; and in Paris the intellectuals, drawn from both the aristocracy and the middle classes, hoped to see English and American freedoms applied to their own country. Jefferson was lionized by Parisian society not merely as a thinker, but also as a practical revolutionary. Paris, however, was hardly representative of the rest of France, and it was in the countryside rather than in the capital that the true malaise was to be found. In 1787 Jefferson spent three months travelling from Paris to Aix-en-Provence. He recorded that:

The people are illy clothed. Perhaps they have put on their worst clothes at the moment as it is raining. But I observe women and children carrying heavy burthens and labouring with the hoe. This is an unequivocal indication of extreme poverty.

Americans were not the only, and perhaps not the deepest, observers of pre-revolutionary France. While Jefferson was on tour in 1787, the English squire, Arthur Young, was beginning the first of three journeys around France that took him the length and breadth of the country. He was only incidentally interested in politics, and the

1   France, 1793.

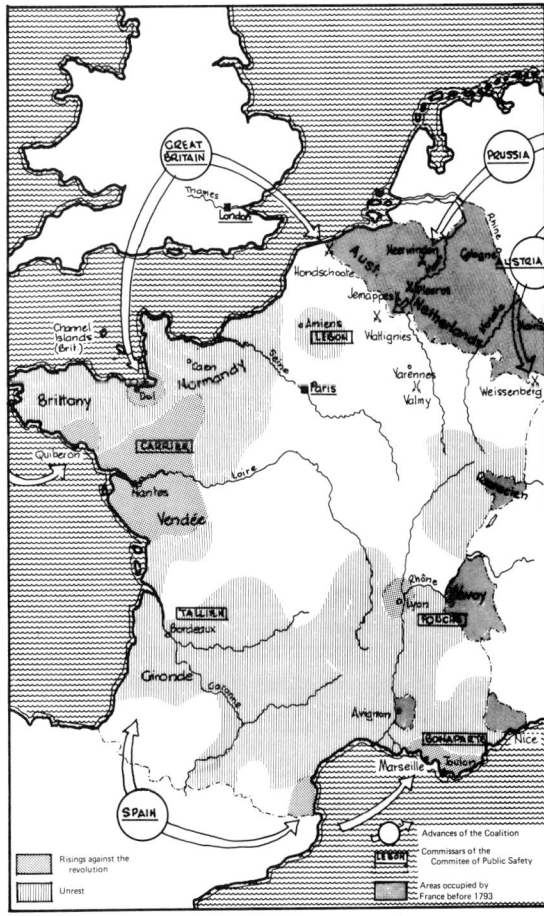

2 A rather romantic view of the eighteenth-century French peasantry, painted by the artist Le Nain. Foreign observers noted that the reality of poverty was often much grimmer.

3 The extravagance of court life is captured in this painting of a ceremony at Reims. Louis XVI, on the left, receives homage from the knights of Saint Esprit.

point of his travels, which he meticulously recorded in his diary, was to observe the state of agriculture in France. The events which he lived through allowed him to observe the first meeting of the Estates General and to watch a revolutionary mob storm Strassbourg town hall; yet, throughout, it was the condition of agriculture and the mass of the people that most interested him. In Limoges in 1787 he met:

a poverty that reminded me of the misery of Ireland . . . . Ploughmen at their work have neither sabots nor feet to their stockings.

In 1788 he was in Montauban:

The poor people seem poor indeed; the children terribly ragged, if possible worse clad than if with no cloaths at all. A beautiful girl of six or seven years . . . smiling under such a bundle of rags as made my heart ache to see her . . . . What have Kings and ministers, and parliaments and states, to answer for their prejudices. I search for good farmers, and run my head at every turn against monks and state prisoners.

The contrast between the town life of the nobility and the poverty of the peasants struck him especially strongly:

What a miracle that all this splendour and wealth of the cities in France should be so unconnected with the country. You move at once from beggary (in mud cabins) to profusion (in theatres).

Indeed, both Jefferson and Young saw the French nobility rather than Louis XVI himself as the real enemy of the people. Jefferson's successor, Gouverneur Morris, concluded that:

[Louis XVI] is an honest man and really wishes to do good, but he has neither genius nor education.

whilst Jefferson had claimed that the King was:

the honestest man in the kingdom . . . he has given repeated proof of a readiness to sacrifice his opinion to the needs of the nation.

Young recorded in 1788 that Louis was more popular than the Parlement, to whom the people attributed the dearness of everything.

Marie Antoinette did not make the same favourable impression. Jefferson wrote:

[The King] had a Queen of absolute sway over his weak mind and tim'd virtue, and of a character the reverse of his in all points. Her inordinate gambling and dissipations, with those of the Count d'Artois [Louis' brother and the future Charles X], have been a sensible item in the exhaustion of the Treasury . . . . The King, long in the habit of drowning his cares in wine, plunges deeper and deeper. The Queen cries but sins on.

Arthur Young said of the nobility that:

They know not how to value the privileges of the people . . . the American revolution has laid the foundation of another in France if government does not take care of itself.

He contrasted their behaviour with that of the English aristocracy. In Paris carriages were driven by:

young men of fashion . . . as to be a real nuisance and render the streets exceedingly dangerous. I saw a poor child run over and probably killed. If young noblemen of London were to drive . . . as their brethren do in Paris, they would speedily and justly get very well thrashed or rolled in the kennel [an open sewer].

The Comte de Mirabeau, when in London, came to the conclusion that the English yeomanry would fight for their aristocracy, because each class recognized the rights and duties of the other; whereas in France, there was a one-sided relationship of exploitation of peasants by the nobility. The French aristocracy, wrote Young:

have no notion of private people going out of their way for the public good . . . the nobility and the King's government seem to have no interest in the land and its people.

On the outbreak of revolution, Morris wrote in a dispatch to President George Washington:

Paris is perhaps as wicked a spot as exists. Incest, murder, bestiality, fraud, rapine, oppression, baseness, cruelty, yet this is the city which has stepped forward in the sacred cause of liberty.

Yet France was potentially one of the wealthiest countries in Europe, with cultural and political achievements second to none; and most informed observers believed that, deep as the crisis was, the regime of Louis XVI could survive, if only it would accept certain minimal reforms. Benjamin Franklin, Jefferson's predecessor as United States ambassador, had seen no irreversible signs of a potential revolution during his tenure of office (1776-85), and, as one of the architects of the American revolution, he might have been expected to recognize a revolutionary situation when he saw it.

An attempt by the King and his ministers to initiate the process of reform by persuading the nobility to undertake a more responsible role had resulted in the 1787 meeting of the Assembly of Notables. The reasons for its failure were seen by Jefferson as symptomatic of the reasons for the government's general failure:

In truth, nothing is known about its object. This government practises secrecy so systematically that it never publishes its purposes.

The Parlement of Paris proved no more effective, and so, in desperation, it was decided to call a meeting of the Estates General for May 1789. While France awaited the occasion, the country suffered a harsh

4 The distrust felt by the common people for the royal family is shown in this cartoon. Louis XVI, pleading poverty, turns away humble suppliants; the royal wealth is cunningly concealed beneath the table.

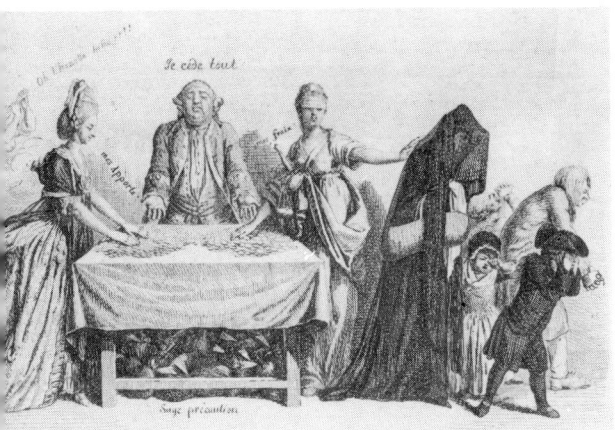

5 When the Estates General met in May 1789, the opulent and formal surroundings of Versailles did not long conceal the deep divisions within French society.

winter. For two months the temperature in Paris registered thirty degrees of frost. The price of bread rose and supplies became short. After a visit to the market of Nangis (near Paris) Young wrote in his diary:

[I] saw the wheat sold with a party of dragoons drawn up before the market to prevent violence, [because] the people quarrel with the bakers, asserting the prices for bread are beyond the proportion of wheat.

It seemed unlikely that the Estates General would be able to solve the problem of food prices. Morris complained on 5 May:

They discuss nothing in the Assembly. One large half of the time is spent in hallowing and bawling – their manner of speaking.

There was a marked lack of inspired and competent leadership. Morris labelled one of the foremost orators of the Third Estate, Mirabeau, as "one of the most unprincipled scoundrels that ever lived"; and Young condemned Abbé Sièyes as a "violent republican". By default, the mantle of public popularity fell on the Duc d'Orleans. Young wrote:

There are palpable and general ideas of distrust and want of confidence, they [the public] regret his character . . . believe him to be without steadiness [but] are so totally without a head, that they look to him as one.

Despite the apparent lack of leadership and new policies, it was the Third Estate of the Estates General that was to become the focal point of the revolution. On 20 June Young wrote:

6 The royal tennis court provided a bizarre setting for the first ominous defiance of royal authority.

News! News! French guards were placed with bayonets to stop any of the deputies entering the [assembly] room. The resolution taken on the spot... was to assemble instantly at the Jeu de paume (tennis court), and there the whole assembly took a solemn oath never to be dissolved.

The Third Estate declared itself to be the National Assembly, and the revolution had begun.

The breakdown in public order that followed was at first sight surprising, as "Versailles seemed filled with troops; the streets were lined with French guards and Swiss regiments". These, however, were not used, even though:

the mob was violent – they insulted and even attacked the clergy and nobility [that wanted to maintain the three separate estates]. The Archbishop of Paris had all his windows broken and the Bishop of Beauvais had a stone on his head that almost struck him down.

Eventually, Young came to realize that the army was not used because:

It is now confidently asserted that if an order was given to the French guards to fire on the people, they will refuse.

The Swiss regiments could have controlled the situation, Young thought, but the King's failure to use them at the outset of the crisis meant that the situation soon escalated out of control. Young concluded:

Lately a company of Swiss would have crushed all this, a regiment would do it now [27 June 1789] if led with firmness; but let it last a fortnight longer and an army will be wanting.

An army would indeed be wanted, but Louis, by then, did not have one.

7 Paris in 1790.

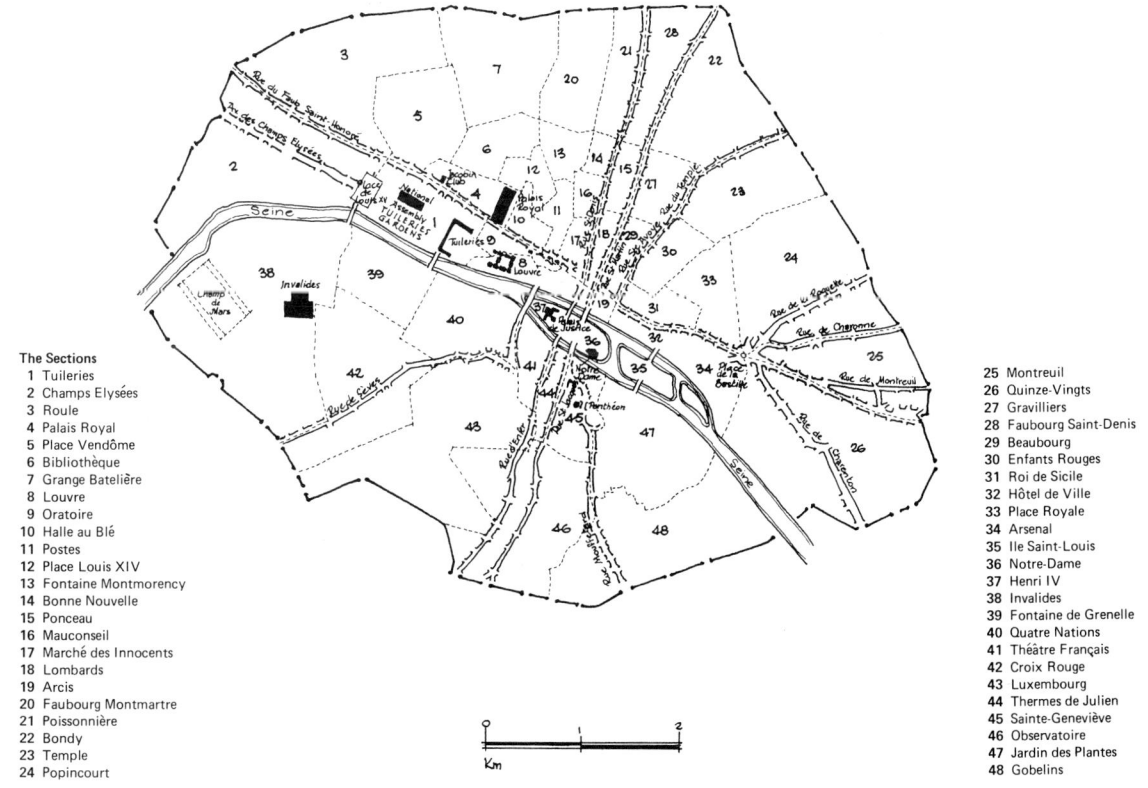

The Sections
1 Tuileries
2 Champs Elysées
3 Roule
4 Palais Royal
5 Place Vendôme
6 Bibliothèque
7 Grange Batelière
8 Louvre
9 Oratoire
10 Halle au Blé
11 Postes
12 Place Louis XIV
13 Fontaine Montmorency
14 Bonne Nouvelle
15 Ponceau
16 Mauconseil
17 Marché des Innocents
18 Lombards
19 Arcis
20 Faubourg Montmartre
21 Poissonnière
22 Bondy
23 Temple
24 Popincourt
25 Montreuil
26 Quinze-Vingts
27 Gravilliers
28 Faubourg Saint-Denis
29 Beaubourg
30 Enfants Rouges
31 Roi de Sicile
32 Hôtel de Ville
33 Place Royale
34 Arsenal
35 Ile Saint-Louis
36 Notre-Dame
37 Henri IV
38 Invalides
39 Fontaine de Grenelle
40 Quatre Nations
41 Théâtre Français
42 Croix Rouge
43 Luxembourg
44 Thermes de Julien
45 Sainte-Geneviève
46 Observatoire
47 Jardin des Plantes
48 Gobelins

The Men Who Made The Revolution

The Third Estate was drawn primarily from men of a frustrated educated middle class, who were excluded from high office and political influence by the system of privilege; over a quarter of them were lawyers. With their allies from the liberal nobility, they dreamed of converting France into a constitutional monarchy on the English model. As late as 1791, most Frenchmen, however critical they might be of the Ancien Régime, believed that a Republic would be the wrong form of government for France.

Revolutions, however, are not made purely by talkative men in assemblies; events in the streets outside often drastically alter the course of events. Peasant unrest, which began with the destruction of feudal records in abbeys and manor houses in the summer of 1789, had led to the total abolition of feudalism by August 1793, although thereafter, except in the Vendée, peasants played little significant part in events. It was from the streets of Paris that the course of the revolution was to be dictated. The riots of 13-14 July 1789, which culminated in the storming of the Bastille; the forceable transfer of the King from Versailles to Paris in October of the same year; and the September massacres in 1792 were all crucial points in the radicalization of the revolution. The culmination came in June 1793, when a hostile demonstration of Parisians, including many National Guard with their cannons, instigated the purging of the Convention and transferred effective absolute power to the Committee of Public Safety. The Parisian activists, commonly known as the "sans-culottes", came largely from the classes of skilled craftsmen and small shopkeepers, the most radical being those of the Faubourg St Antoine. As in the winter and spring of 1788-89, economic grievances were often the trigger. The vital events of June 1793 and July 1794 took place against a background of shortages and inflation.

Pressure from Paris, the failure of Louis XVI to co-operate consistently in the construction of a constitutional regime, and the threat of foreign invasion, all combined to cause power to fall increasingly into the hands of politicians who were willing to abandon their earlier caution and adopt more radical policies. Robespierre, who had earlier resigned his post as a judge in the provinces because he could not bear to inflict the death penalty, was willing by 1792 to canvas for the execution of the King. Some of these extremist politicians were genuine idealists, like Robespierre, Saint-Just and, perhaps, Carrier – disciples of Rousseau, who believed that they alone knew what was good for France, saw opposition as selfish, sinister and treacherous, and thought any means justified in order to ensure the future. In one of his last speeches, Robespierre said:

The government of the revolution is the despotism of liberty against tyranny. Must might be used only to protect crime?

Others who climbed to power were men whose ambitions or grudges against the old social system had made them eager to carve careers and reputations out of upheaval. Collot d'Herbois, member of the Committee of Public Safety and brutal suppressor of the Lyons counter-revolution, had been an actor and had suffered the social ostracism that went with his profession. Hébert, editor of the scurrilous and influential *Père Duchesne*, had come to Paris to seek his fortune, become the manager of a theatre box-office, and been sacked even from that lowly job. Nicholas Guenot (page 26) was a man of similar stamp.

The old royalist army provided many recruits for the revolution. Before 1789 no common soldier, however competent, could hope to become an officer. In his history of the French revolution, published in 1837, Thomas Carlyle wrote:

> By the law . . . no man can pretend to be the pitifullest Lieutenant of Militia till he first have verified, to the satisfaction of the Lion King [expert on heraldry], a nobility of four generations.

Napoleon on St Helena referred to the frustrations generated by this rule as one of the chief causes of the revolution. Lazare Carnot, military expert on the Committee of Public Safety and "organizer of victory", had his brilliant career in the engineering corps blocked at the rank of captain, and became a staunch convert to the principles of republicanism. The successful French armies of 1793 and 1794 were commanded by generals whose loyalty to the Republic was guaranteed by the opportunities it had given them to rise from the ranks. Eight of the future Marshals of Napoleon – Massena, Murat, Victor, Oudinot, Soult, Ney, Lefebvre and Bernadotte – were from this group.

Jean-Baptiste Humbert

Jean-Baptiste Humbert was the first to climb on to the towers of the Bastille. A watchmaker of the St André district of Paris, he was a member of that class of craftsmen and shopkeepers who did so much to give momentum to the revolution. While most of them remain anonymous, Humbert has left an account, counter-signed by five eye-witnesses, of his role in the seizure of the Bastille.

As a skilled craftsman, Humbert had reasonable prospects; he was eager to emphasize that he was no hooligan nor lover of violence, but a man of political principle:

> In all my endeavours I so firmly believed that I was only doing my duty that I sought to gain neither glory nor profit therefrom, and was happy to earn six francs a day in my profession until I should have established myself, but happier still to have helped France recover her liberty and to have given some pleasure to my relatives by the story of my actions.

His love of liberty and hatred of monarchical tyranny stemmed from the days of his apprenticeship in Geneva, where he had witnessed in 1782 the overthrow of the Genevan Republic by French troops:

> I witnessed the dismay of the townspeople and heard the curses they uttered against a certain minister of France . . . . I heard so many sighs, complaints and regrets that for a long time I have in my heart something of the same feeling as the unfortunate people of Geneva.

On 12 July 1789, when rumours circulated in Paris of the approach of royalist troops ordered to suppress all dissent, Humbert joined an impromptu defence force made up of a cross-section of the citizens of St André, which was soon to become the St André division of the National Guard. Few had any firearms, and when Humbert discovered that arms were being distributed at the royal armoury of Les Invalides, he persuaded his

8 The capture of the Bastille is often depicted as a heroic and bloodthirsty event. In fact, few shots were fired and the fortress surrendered almost without a fight.

comrades to go and get their share. On their arrival, they found chaos. The King's indecisiveness had completely demoralized the defenders and they had opened up the weapon store to the public; no one, however, had undertaken to organize the distribution. The arms were kept in a cellar, but:

the crowd at the top of the stair was so great that all those who were climbing up were pushed down again and fell right into the cellar.

In the chaos, Humbert was separated from his companions, but managed to acquire a musket and set off back to St André. On the way:

I learned that they were handing out powder at the Hotel de Ville [town hall]. I hurried thither and was given about half a pound, but they gave me no shot, saying that they had none.

Humbert, however, was ever resourceful:

As I left the Hotel de Ville I heard someone saying that the Bastille was being besieged. My regret at having no shot prompted an idea which I immediately carried out, namely to buy some small nails, which I got from the grocer's at the Coin du Roi by the Place de Grève. There I fixed up and greased my gun.

As a shopkeeper, Humbert was terrified that the revolution might degenerate into general disorder and looting of property. En route for the Bastille, he went to the aid of a woman whose saltpetre shop was about to be set on fire:

I found a barber holding a lighted torch in each hand, with which he was indeed setting fire to the place. I rushed at the barber and thrust the butt of my gun violently against his stomach, knocking him over. Then, seeing that the barrel of saltpetre had caught fire, I overturned it and succeeded in smothering the flames.

At the Bastille, Humbert took a leading role. The drawbridge was already lowered when he arrived, but the portcullis was still closed:

People were trying to bring in some cannon which had previously been dismantled. I dashed over . . . and helped to bring in the two guns. When they had been set up on their gun carriages, everybody with one accord drew up in rows of five or six and I found myself in the front rank.

It proved unnecessary to fire the cannon, however, for, almost immediately, the demoralized Swiss Guard surrendered the fortress. Humbert was one of the first through the gate and helped disarm the Swiss – not a difficult task as the following extract shows:

In the keep I found a Swiss soldier squatting down with his back to me. I aimed my rifle at him shouting, "Lay down your arms". He turned round in surprise and laid down his weapons saying, "Comrade, don't kill me; I'm for the Third Estate and I will defend you to the last drop of my blood; you know I'm obliged to do my job, but I haven't fired.

Humbert's enthusiasm and initiative then nearly brought him into danger:

Immediately afterwards I went to the cannon that stood just above the drawbridge of the Bastille, in order to push it off its gun carriage and render it unusable. But as I stood for this purpose with my shoulder under the mouth of the cannon, someone in the vicinity fired at me, and the bullet pierced my coat and waistcoat and wounded me in the neck. I fell down senseless.

Humbert revived, to find himself being tended by the Swiss whose life he had saved, an action that nearly cost the latter his life, for:

Half way down the stairs we met a crowd of townsfolk coming up . . . seeing me covered in blood, they assumed that the Swiss must have wounded me and tried to kill him. I opposed them and explained the situation. They fortunately took my word for it.

After having his wound dressed at a monastery, Humbert returned home to rest, but his excitement at being a participant in momentous events would not leave him. He recalls:

I rested until about midnight, when I was woken by repeated cries of "to arms, to arms!" Then I could not resist my longing to be of further use; I got up, armed myself and went to the guardroom, where I found M. Poirier, the commanding officer, under whose orders I remained until the following morning.

9 Popular imagination painted the prisoners released from the Bastille as martyrs and victims of a corrupt regime. In fact, its dungeons contained only four forgers, two lunatics, one dissolute nobleman, and *no* political detainees. The significance of the event was purely symbolic, establishing the victory of the people of Paris over the royal government.

Here Humbert's account ends. It would be intriguing to know whether he remained active in Parisian politics and what his feelings were as the revolution fell into the hands of an increasingly violent minority. However, no trace of his subsequent activities can be discovered.

Honoré Gabriel Riqueti, Comte de Mirabeau (1749-91)

Mirabeau exemplifies that small group of nobles who, briefly, controlled the early course of the revolution. A man of contradictions, he died at a crucial moment. For two years he had tried to serve both the revolution and the monarchy; if he had lived longer, he would have perhaps become a victim himself.

From youth, Mirabeau had aroused strong feelings. "He has a gross-grained mind, is fantastic, impetuous, troublesome, with a tendency to evil", wrote his father when Mirabeau was only twelve. Yet he could arouse strong attractions, especially in women: when he was fifteen, his tutor wrote to his father, "His ways have already forced me to dismiss two maids". At eighteen, a love affair with a police official's daughter resulted in his running away from the regiment, to which he had been sent to help him mend his

10 Mirabeau, a caricature by David.

ways. An uncle summed him up:

He is either the biggest humbug in the world, or the person in Europe best suited to become a general ... or a minister.

For the next twenty years Mirabeau was either in prison, held under the infamous system of "lettres de cachet", or leading the life of a penniless adventurer, disowned by his family. During this time he wrote political tracts and served as a secret agent, travelling throughout Europe and meeting politicians such as the former French finance ministers Necker (who became an enemy) and Calonne. Without the events of 1789, he would probably have died in obscurity, but in 1788 he wrote prophetically:

Should a revolution or a civil war break out in France, I tremble for the aristocratic branches of the kingdom. Their chateaux will be reduced to ashes, and blood will be spilt in torrents.

His function, he believed, would be to control such events. As early as 1788, he wrote to Talleyrand about the Assembly of Notables: "I see in it a new order of things which can regenerate the monarchy". On hearing of the summoning of the Estates General, Mirabeau declared: "The country has gone forward a century in twenty-four hours".

Mirabeau made it his goal to become a member of the Estates General. Foiled in his attempt to represent the First Estate, he reluctantly turned to the Third. He was elected simultaneously for two different constituencies, Marseilles and Aix-en-Provence, having helped in both towns to quell riots, using no more than his personal charisma; and soon he became the self-selected "spokesman of the nation" to the King. His actions in June 1789 were crucial in creating the National Assembly. To the Marquis de Brézé, who attempted to dismiss the Third Estate, Mirabeau ordered:

Go and say to your master that we are here by the will of the people, and that we will not be put out except by the force of bayonets.

After the fall of the Bastille, he urged the dismissal of the King's ministers, and in so doing rejected his own class, saying: "I attach so little importance to my title of count that I give it to whomever wishes it". Yet he remained a monarchist, and in a letter to the courtier La Marck, who acted as a link between King and Assembly, he wrote: "Take care at the Palace that they know I am with them rather than against them".

As his reputation in the Assembly grew, Mirabeau became convinced that he was the man of the hour:

The Monarchy is in danger rather because no-one governs than because anyone conspires. If no pilot presents himself, the vessel will run aground [but if] a man of brains [is] called upon, you cannot imagine how easy it would be to put the vessel afloat again.

Many in the Assembly were determined that the pilot should not be Mirabeau, and thought him to be a self-seeking orator. The Marquis de Ferriers said:

> To the natural talents that make great orators, Mirabeau added a careful study of the art of oratory. He knew that the man of genius appeals more to the feelings than to reason. Therefore, his gestures, his look and the sound of his voice were all based upon a profound knowledge of the human heart.

Mirabeau's hopes of office were dashed, when the Assembly passed a self-denying ordinance, excluding any of its membership from becoming a minister. Mirabeau retorted ironically: "Let me propose the amendment; that the suggested exclusion be confined to M. de Mirabeau".

Perhaps the bitterness which he now felt can explain why, henceforth, Mirabeau increasingly abandoned his role of champion of the Assembly and began to conspire with the King. He proceeded to "make it my chief business to see that the executive power has its place in the constitution"; in return, his many debts were to be paid for him by Louis:

> If, as he promises, M. de Mirabeau serves me well . . . he will receive a million. Meanwhile, I will see that his debts are paid and you yourself will decide what sum I should give him monthly.
> (Letter from Louis XVI to La Marck. The sum eventually agreed was 6,000 livres per month).

It is impossible to be certain whether these payments now caused Mirabeau to become "a traitor to the revolution", as the Jacobin pamphlet *Trahison Decouverte du Comte de Mirabeau* claimed. The well-disposed Lafayette claimed that "Mirabeau would not for any sum have supported an opinion destructive of liberty or dishonourable to his mind"; but others in the Third Estate, such as Rivarol, had a lower opinion of Mirabeau – "capable of anything for money, even of a good action". Mirabeau himself was reported to have told Lameth that "I am not entirely my own master".

However, it *is* clear that the court did not pay much attention to his advice, as many around Louis thought him to be too much of a revolutionary to be trusted. It remains impossible to judge whether the French people on the death of Mirabeau lost a great statesman who never had the chance to show his skills as a minister. Mirabeau on his death bed in April 1791 believed that they had:

> I go wearing mourning for the monarchy; after my death the factions will fight over the shreds.

And the people of Paris agreed, for it was Mirabeau who was first buried in the Panthéon – a former church building converted into a shrine, dedicated to great men of the revolution. However, the ambiguity of his reputation soon became apparent. When the Tuileries were invaded and the documents outlining his relationship with the King became public knowledge, he was disinterred and re-buried in a public grave. Perhaps the final words on this enigmatic character could be those of Gouverneur Morris in April 1791:

> I have seen this man in the short space of two years hissed, honoured, hated, mourned. Enthusiasm has just now made him gigantic. Time and reflection will change that.

11 At his death, Mirabeau was acclaimed as a champion of popular liberty. In this contemporary painting, "Mirabeau arrive aux Champs Elysées", he is placed in the company of the great philosophers, past and present, including Rousseau, Voltaire, Cicero and Demosthenes. His reputation, however, did not remain long unsullied.

Louis-Antoine de Saint-Just (1768-94)

Saint-Just's public career was limited entirely to the period of the revolution. A young man of only twenty-seven when he died, he felt:

> within me something that triumphs with the age . . . . Because I am young I think I am close to nature and the true feelings of the people. (1794)

His greatest fear was that the revolution would pass him by. The events of 1789-91 left him a frustrated observer, following the career of country lawyer that had been chosen for him by his mother. He had certainly not wished to become a respectable bourgeois, and at the age of eighteen had stolen the family silver and run away to Paris to earn his living by pen or sword. Both pursuits eluded him and he was held in prison, at his mother's request, until he agreed to begin legal studies. Coincidentally, the law school that he attended at Rheims numbered among its graduates Brissot and Danton.

In 1789 he was in Paris again, this time as a visitor. Here he met Camille Desmoulins, but could find no part to play in Parisian politics. He returned to Blérancourt, joined the National Guard there, and set out to make his mark in local politics. His sole claim to fame at this time was a letter that he wrote to Robespierre, on behalf of the local poor – a letter that Robespierre kept and which marked the beginnings of their friendship. Saint-Just's feelings of frustration were immense and he sublimated them in writing *Spirit of the Revolution* (1791). The treatise contained nothing new, but the freshness of its approach made it a bestseller, and, partly on the strength of this, Saint-Just was elected to the National Assembly. Even this success proved illusory. At twenty-two he was declared under-age and forced to give up his seat; he even lost his electoral rights. 1791 saw Saint-Just at his lowest ebb, and, with Robespierre, he could say: "The revolution is

12 Saint-Just.

ended".

However, events in Paris precipitated the revolution into a new stage. The publication of the Brunswick Manifesto on 25 July 1792, the storming of the Tuileries and the Assembly's decision to summon a National Convention to decide the fate of Louis XVI, allowed Saint-Just to step on to the national stage, when he was elected to the Convention in September 1792. This time his sense of mission – "To found the Republic of his dreams he would have given his head and a hundred thousand heads with it" (René Levasseur, 1879) – was to find an outlet. The Jacobins, with their motto "La force de la raison et la force du peuple, c'est la même chose", were his obvious fellow-thinkers and Saint-Just took his place amongst the Mountain.

Once elected, Saint-Just wasted no time in making a name for himself, and Marat was to call him "the only orator who has afforded me any pleasure". Saint-Just's first target was the King, who, he believed, should be executed. In November 1792 Saint-Just argued: "It is impossible to reign and be innocent". Despite the pressure of the Paris mob, not all the Convention agreed, and moderates urged that:

We must be free to say to posterity that it was the whole of France and not the people of Paris that judged Louis XVI.

Such views were dismissed by Saint-Just, as merely proving that monarchism was still alive, and he had no doubt that "if I did not hold from the people the right to judge the tyrant, I would hold it from nature".

The subsequent execution of Louis XVI had the polarizing effect that so many Jacobins desired. For the revolution to survive against the hostility of Europe, it had to become more extreme. It might even be argued that disasters such as the defection of Dumouriez and the counter-revolution in the Vendée were welcomed as giving a legitimate excuse for the destruction of "traitors" (i.e. moderates) in the republican government. Saint-Just's attitude is illustrated by the following extract from a speech he made in 1793:

One does not make revolution by halves . . . . I know of but one method of resisting Europe, and that is to oppose to it the genius of liberty.

In 1793 the Committee of Public Safety was created to deal with the crisis, and for a while Danton was dominant. In May of that year Saint-Just was one of five new members co-opted on to the Committee for the specific task of drafting a new constitution for France – with an eight-day deadline. This completed, Saint-Just moved on to help create policy, and in November 1793 was the author of a report accusing the Girondins of plotting counter-revolution. Danton fell from power, and with the sponsorship of Carnot and Robespierre, Saint-Just came into his own. Some considered he had come too far, too fast, and was too arrogant and self-righteous. Desmoulins complained:

13 Fanatical Jacobins like Saint-Just believed that they alone were true patriots – "le patriote exclusif", shown in this cartoon.

One gathers from his bearing that he considers his head the cornerstone of the Republic, and he carries it on his shoulders with reverence, as if it were the Holy Sacrament.

The ex-actor, Collot d'Herbois accused him of being "nothing but a box of aphorisms".

14 The Girondins, once revolutionary comrades, were among the victims of Saint-Just's fanaticism.

Saint-Just had enough confidence in his sense of mission to ignore such criticisms:

Those who make revolutions in the world, those who wish to win to better things, must not sleep except in the tomb.

Military set-backs saw Saint-Just dispatched to the front, where he saw counter-revolutionaries within the Republican ranks as the true enemy. He and his friend Le Bas created a military tribunal for the Army of the Rhine, and in four months it dealt with 660 cases, condemning 62 people to death. They next transferred their attentions to the Army of the North. The Terror was not merely a weapon to Saint-Just; it was an essential part of the Revolution. Without it, morale would weaken, and the counter-revolutionaries would win. In March 1794 Saint-Just and Robespierre eliminated members of the revolutionary leadership with whom they had fallen into disagreement. Among those executed was Danton.

Danton (thundered Saint-Just), you are answerable to an inevitable and inflexible justice . . . we will prove that since the first day . . . you have been the enemy of the party of liberty, that you plotted with Mirabeau, with Dumouriez and with Hérault de Séchelles.

Even Saint-Just's own colleagues lived in fear of his denunciations. Carrier and Fouché, out of favour since the massacres at Nantes and Lyons, were afraid to visit their own homes and slept at a different house every night.

Its advocates believed that the Terror was necessary for the survival of the Republic. 1794, however, saw the tide of war turning in France's favour, and, ironically, success made the Terror, and hence Saint-Just and Robespierre, less necessary. In the plot of Thermidor (26-27 July) disgruntled Jacobins avoided their own elimination by engineering the arrest of Robespierre, Saint-Just, Couthon and Le Bas. Le Bas shot himself, but the others were guillotined on the Place de la Révolution where Louis XVI had died eighteen months before. Saint-Just submitted indifferently and in silence. A Thermidorian pamphlet rejoiced:

Vive la République! The tyrants are no more. Robespierre, Couthon and Saint-Just can no longer put you in chains. They have expiated their crimes and their parricidal heads have just fallen on the scaffold.

Jean-Baptiste Carrier (1756-94)

Elected to the National Convention as the deputy for the Cantal region, Carrier's reputation as a staunch Jacobin caused him to be sent as Representative on Mission to Normandy, in July 1793. A Girondist uprising in the area had just been defeated, and Carrier's brief was to co-ordinate efforts for the elimination of all anti-government elements. At the end of September, he was sent on a similar mission to Nantes. With the royalist Vendéan revolt at its height, Nantes remained one of the few Republican strongholds in the West, and the centre where captured rebels were incarcerated.

To Carrier's unstinting efforts must go some of the credit for the Republic's eventual victory in the West, but it was a victory achieved at great cost. Carrier instructed his generals to "burn, burn continuously", and the Vendée was systematically laid waste. It

15 Although Carrier is best known for his part in the mass drownings in the Loire, the more traditional guillotine was also active during his mission at Nantes.

was the massacre at Nantes, however, that sealed Carrier's infamous reputation among both contemporaries and historians. In November 1793 boatloads of prisoners, roped together, were drowned in the Loire. The exact numbers involved cannot be verified, but the drowning of children is well-attested, as are the activities of one executioner, who cut off the arms of victims as they struggled to escape from the river. Carrier defended his actions as necessary for the safety of the Republic, but his behaviour was condemned at the time, even by those who normally put the security of the Republic above humanitarian considerations. Among historians, his reputation is universally black. Alfred Cobban writes:

16 The blackness of Carrier's reputation has seldom been challenged. In this 1839 engraving, he is shown as a heartless monster condemning women and children.

17 Carrier and his fellow Jacobins preferred to see themselves as heroic and incorruptible defenders of the people.

After Robespierre, he [Carrier] became the symbol of the Terror, and there was little need to blacken his reputation as Robespierre's had been blackened. (*A History of Modern France*, Vol I, Pelican, 1957)

Yet there was little indication in Carrier's earlier life of such ruthlessness. Employed as a town clerk before 1789, he earned a reputation as a conscientious, hardworking lawyer, who was affable, generous with money and fond of animals and children. His work in Normandy earned him praise from St André of the Committee of Public Safety, as a steady patriot, whose judgement could be relied on. Even in the midst of the Nantese bloodbath, he proved a generous friend to the few he really trusted. With the Committee in Paris he pleaded the case of an army surgeon who wanted the youngest of his seven sons transferred to his own regiment:

Will the Convention agree to authorise a displacement, prohibited by law, in favour of a venerable man who is consecrating his latter days and those of his children to his country's defence?

Why, then, did this once reasonable man turn to a career of apparently mindless violence?

At the start of his mission, Carrier was given almost unlimited power and encouraged to be ruthless in his pursuit of enemies of the Republic. His friend Hérault de Séchelles wrote in August 1793:

So that's how things are going, good old friend! . . I have just received your letter and at the same moment I read it to the Committee of Public Safety; its members heard it with marked satisfaction. We ourselves would be extremely glad, and the Republic vigorous and flourishing, if everywhere there were agents as energetic as you and your colleagues. We are sending you an order to authorise you to purge the town as a matter of the utmost importance.

It would have needed exceptional strength of character to exercise such power with restraint, and Carrier was to prove temperamentally unsuited to the wielding of what was, in practice, absolute power.

He believed fervently in the Jacobin cause and refused to see merit in any view but his own. He wrote of his stay in St Malo (Brittany) at the end of July:

I have thoroughly stirred up men's minds. We hear no cries but those of the most ardent patriotism. 'Vive la République, Vive la Montaigne, Vivent les Sansculottes'. These are the only acclamations that echo from the walls of St Malo. Every evening after the sitting of the Popular Society, citizens of both sexes, nearly all the population of St Malo, accompany me home, chanting patriotic hymns; a little while, I flatter myself . . . I shall have thoroughly sansculottised those citizens whom perfidious persons, together with journalists subsidised by the aristocracy, have led into error.

Increasingly, Carrier saw himself as single-handedly responsible for the conversion of the West to true Jacobinism.

At Nantes, the over-conscientious Carrier soon became overworked and harassed. In November, the Committee instructed him to ensure the loyalty of Nantese Republicans throughout the winter by adequately provisioning the city. Carrier complained:

Further I would draw your attention to the fact that one Representative cannot look after this and the crowds of other extremely important matters in his care.

His health deteriorated under the strain. As early as September he could write: "The work has strangely broken down my health. Yesterday I was very ill". Evidently, ill-health was chronic throughout the period in question for in January he postponed a visit to the battlefront until "my health is established and my lungs have gained new force".

In November, Vendéan rebels, defeated at Glanville, fell back towards Nantes, causing hysteria in the city; rumours circulated of a mass breakout from the prisons and the massacre of known Republicans. In fragile mental and physical health, faced with the ruin of all he had thus far achieved, Carrier disposed of the problem of the prisoners in what was to be the swiftest and simplest means available – the mass drowning in the Loire.

Carrier seems to have suffered a total breakdown by January 1794. While his agents tyrannized the countryside, he shut himself up in his lodgings and refused to see even his colleagues. A deputation sent to inquire after his health by the Popular Society of Vincent la Montaigne (a Jacobin club of a small town near Nantes) later sent him a letter of complaint:

How are they received at your house, these free men, who believe themselves your friends and brothers? Your door is closed to them and a secretary . . . tells them that were they patriots come from the dead, they could not speak with you.

It was reported to the Committee of Public

Safety that his agents "pillaged, burned and killed without restraint", victimizing rebels and loyal patriots indiscriminately. In February he was recalled.

On his return to Paris, finding himself ostracized by the Committee, Carrier retaliated by joining with other malcontents to oust Robespierre. When the events of Thermidor resulted in a backlash against all Jacobins, those with a reputation for vigorous pro-Jacobinism sought to melt into obscurity. Some succeeded; Carrier did not. Denounced as a "cannibal", he admitted his guilt, exonerated his colleagues as mere agents, and died bravely.

Carrier is a type familiar in revolutions. Decent men in private life, they are thrown by political upheaval into positions of great authority over their fellow citizens. Heady with unaccustomed power, sincere, dedicated and overworked, they lose sight of their humanity. Perhaps the best summary of Carrier's career is that of the American historian, R.R. Palmer:

Carrier, it may safely be said, was a normal man, with average sensibilities and with no unusual intelligence or strength of character, driven wild by opposition, turning ruthless because ruthlessness seemed to be the easiest way of solving a difficult problem. (*Twelve Who Ruled*, Princeton University Press, 1941).

Paul de Thiebault (1770-1846)

In Paris, in July 1789, the National Guard was formed. Its leaders came primarily from the middle classes and the liberal nobility, who sympathized with the early aims of the revolution and wanted to prevent a counter-attack by royalist forces, but who also feared the anarchy and bloodshed that might flow from the unchecked enthusiasm of the artisans of Paris. Paul de Thiebault, son of a minor French nobleman, was disillusioned enough with the Ancien Régime to welcome the events of July 1789, and later recalled the youthful desire to be at the centre of momentous events that led him to join the National Guard at its foundation:

While puzzling myself as to what my father would think, how vexed my mother would be, I considered that I was not old enough to attach myself to what must be the falling cause; that at nineteen years old one belongs to the attacking party; and that I personally owed nothing to anyone. From that moment nothing could have weakened the feeling of what I owed my country, and as the result of this rapid cogitation, I replied, "I am with you." (*Memoirs of General Thiebault*, 1817-20)

Complete amateurs in the art of soldiering, Thiebault's troop set off to requisition arms from Les Invalides:

Our troop had nothing military about it but its courage; no discipline save its zeal; its strength was only that of five hundred times that of one man, a very different thing from what the strength of five hundred men may be; we went along rather than marched.

After this, an attempt was made to organize the National Guard on a proper military footing and Thiebault was given command of 600 men; he owed his promotion purely to the fact that he was able to impress his superiors with his ability to quote the military maxims of Frederick the Great, which he had learnt at school. On a reconnoitre of a Paris suburb they nearly ran into trouble with an equally amateurish troop:

We went tranquilly along the road, and had traversed half of it, when a great uproar was heard in front of us. However, having amid so many shouts made out that of "Who goes there?", I hastened to reply, "Parisian Guard, Feuillants District". The noise changed its character without diminishing; some men, plucky fellows, no doubt, came running up to look at us and called out at once, "Do not fire". I could not understand it, but at last it appeared that they had taken us for troops from the Champs de Mars coming to suppress the Roule district, and that if the match [fuse] lying near the two pieces [of cannon] that were trained up our road had not happened to go out, we would have been met with a salute from two twelve-pounders loaded with grape.

With time, however, the National Guard developed an esprit de corps that turned it into an efficient fighting force. Within months:

there was such community of feeling among us that something extraordinary must have happened for any of us to fail in turning up for the roll-call.

By 1792 Thiebault was thoroughly alarmed by the excesses of the sans-culottes who were gaining control in Paris. Of the events of 10 August he wrote:

After the 10th August, with its decisive triumph of crime and murder, it was no longer the same revolution which I had intended to serve and to which I had been proud to sacrifice so many interests.

But he despised the emigrés even more and, as a patriotic Frenchman, regarded with horror the threat of foreign invasion. He solved his dilemma by enlisting as a foot-soldier in one of the volunteer battalions then being raised to stiffen the regular army on France's Eastern frontier. He told a fellow volunteer: "Paris is no longer habitable; the country is in danger;

18 The July 1792 declaration of "La Patrie en Danger" caused volunteers from all walks of life to enrol enthusiastically for military service. This amateur army was to win notable victories against the professional armies of Europe.

I shall go and enlist."

In keeping with the new spirit of equality, each company of volunteers was entitled to select its own officers. The choice of Thiebault's group was unfortunate. Captain Bertaux was a professional engraver who specialized in battle scenes; he panicked during the first engagement:

He had his sword on the wrong side, only one glove, a straw hat; his countenance was perturbed, and he could not remember a single word of command.

Second-in-command, Lieutenant Odiot, was a jeweller with a shop in the Rue St Honoré; after four months he returned to Paris to look after his business. The sub-lieutenant was a violinist who later became musical director of the Italian opera; surprisingly, he proved to be a competent soldier. Thiebault recalls that they were chosen, "largely because the idea of holding any rank with the responsibility it implied frightened the greater number". In such circumstances, discipline under fire was hard to maintain. In one skirmish a hare was disturbed and instantly:

The enemy was forgotten and two hundred men dashed after the hare, firing, prodding with bayonets, striking with butts, at the risk of killing or wounding one another. In spite of all the officers could say or do, this absurd chase continued, amid shouts, peels of laughter, and general amazement on the part of the Austrians, till the unlucky beast was in the knapsack of one of the pursuers.

Food supplies were erratic; at one point, troops were reduced to "half a ration of mouldy bread and two ounces of rancid bacon". The only compensation for such conditions was that they affected the enemy equally. Of the campaign after the Battle of Valmy, Thiebault writes:

Say what anyone will about the mud of Champagne, it is hard to form an idea of what it was like that autumn. The open country was quite impracticable; the roads, washed by continual rain and broken up by the movements of so many armies, were covered by five or six inches of slush in which I marched whole hours without seeing my feet. But that mud, that climate, the days of downpour, combined with a want of provisions and with the grapes plucked from our vines, had given us a terrible ally against the Prussians, who had been decimated by dysentery.

A few months of such conditions wrecked Thiebault's health. After one enforced rest he tried to rejoin his regiment "but the weather kept getting colder and I began to spit blood and was obliged to stop". When he had totally recovered in February 1793 Thiebault rejoined the regular army as a lieutenant and experienced at first hand the new Republican system of appointing senior officers. Until the end of 1792 most commanders had been inherited from the old royalist officers corps. Soon after the defection of Dumouriez, a decree of the Convention expelled from the army all persons of noble birth. Thereafter, officers were promoted from the ranks, on the basis of merit, and the Representatives on Mission were charged with selecting the right men. Thiebault observed that:

The representatives to the armies cashiered, superseded and arrested at their pleasure officers of any rank, creating new ones, until

19 In spite of its amateurish beginnings, the Revolutionary Army won some spectacular and unexpected victories against the experienced Austrian and Prussian armies. After the Battle of Jemappes, November 1792, the Republic occupied Belgium.

privates or even drummers became at a bound brigadiers, major generals or generals of division. One may instance Ballard, who had been the drummer of my company at the Feuillants, a man of neither style nor substantive merit, but who found himself, on a sudden, general of division.

Thiebault's new commander, Charbonnier, was such a field promotion, and, although personally brave, won his subordinate's contempt, so that "but for my father I should have left the service".

In retrospect, Thiebault was convinced that only luck prevented the total defeat of the French armies in 1793:

How many times has it been repeated . . . that without generals, without officers, without soldiers, we beat the armies of all the world. Nothing could be more ridiculous or more untrue. But for the systematic slowness of the Austrians, we should have been beaten ninety nine times out of a hundred. They alone save us by giving us time to make soldiers, officers and generals.

Eventually, however, experience turned volunteers into soldiers and the revolutionary promotion system proved its worth, for:

While the delegates raised to the higher grades

men of little use or worth, they also brought forward some of high ability and force, like Hoche, Marceau, Kleber... Jourdain, Massena, not to mention the hero among heroes, the great man among so many great men [Napoleon].

As a member of the nobility, albeit a minor one, Thiebault himself narrowly escaped arrest during the Terror of the Year II. He survived to become a general by the age of thirty, to serve in the campaigns in Italy and Portugal, to fight at Austerlitz and to write a manual of military instruction that is still read by military historians. Like that of many more famous names, Thiebault's illustrious career owed much to the opportunities opened up by the Republic's abolition of the barriers of age and class in the armed forces.

Jacques-Louis David (1748-1825)

At the outset of the revolution, David was already the most celebrated French painter of his day and the exponent of a new artistic trend. He despised the pretty and frivolous subjects popular at the beginning of the century and replaced them with an austere style copied from classical sculpture. His favourite topics were the virtues of ancient Greece and Rome – patriotism, heroism and self-sacrifice. In 1785, his "Oath of the Horatii", in which three young Romans are taking an oath on their father's sword to defeat the enemy or die in the struggle, became the fashionable painting of its day. His reputation was such that, while his future colleague Fouché was earning 80 livres per annum as a teacher, David could command a fee of 300 livres for a routine portrait of the Mayor of Nantes. Forty-two years-old in 1789, a member of the prestigious Royal Academy and patronized by the aristocracy, David could look forward to a lifetime of wealth and success under the Ancien Régime.

David has left no personal explanation of his political opinions, but with such a background it is surely safe to assume that his instant devotion to the Jacobin cause was sincere and disinterested. Contemporaries believed that his artistic obsession with the themes of ancient history had converted the artist to Republicanism; it is impossible to be certain of the validity of this evaluation, although it is clear that David was a man who could do nothing by halves; once he had decided to adopt the revolutionary cause, he did so in the most spectacular way open to him. David's activity on behalf of the revolution took two forms: he used his artistic skills to produce propaganda, and he took an active role in day-to-day politics.

Canvasses of the dramatic events of revolutionary history were commissioned from David, including a giant painting (never completed) of the Tennis Court Oath, which was then to be engraved and mass-produced. It was announced in the Assembly:

Considering that the 20th June is the epoch that assured France of a free constitution... David's picture will be completed at the expense of the public treasury and will be placed in the meeting place of the National Assembly.

David was more than willing to use his talent in this way. When Marat's death was announced in the Convention, a deputy from Paris cried, "Where are you, David? You have given posterity the image of Le Peletier [another assassinated Republican leader]: there still remains a picture to be done."

20 David – the ardent revolutionary, who became court-painter to Napoleon.

21 David was an eye-witness to many of the great events of the revolution. From a window, he sketched Marie Antoinette on her way to the guillotine.

David replied, "I will not forget." The great Republican festivals, which were intended to act as unifying forces and fill the gap left by the abolition of the monarchy and the decline of religion, and which Robespierre hoped would "mould the souls of citizens in the way of virtue, that is to say, in the love of fatherland and liberty", were masterminded by David, who became designated by history as the "pageant-master of the Revolution". When proposing a competition to design a colossal statue for the Pont Neuf, symbolizing the French people, David justified his involvement in such propaganda activities:

Each of us is accountable to the Fatherland for the talents which he has received from nature... the true patriot ought to seize with avidity every means of enlightening his fellow citizens, and of presenting ceaselessly to their eyes the sublime traits of heroism and virtue.

The culmination came at the Festival of the Supreme Being in June 1794, which marked the official replacement of Christianity by the worship of Nature. In front of huge crowds, Robespierre set fire, with a torch handed to him by the designer, David, to a huge cardboard figure of Atheism, which burnt away to reveal the figure of Wisdom. The entire Convention, along with selected Parisians, then climbed on to an artificial mountain erected on the Champs de Mars, where patriotic songs were sung and girls threw white flowers. David and his colleagues obviously saw nothing ridiculous in such ceremonies, although one sceptical contemporary described it as "the most foolish, abominable and ridiculous activity that was ever seen in Paris".

Apart from works of propaganda, David also produced a series of graphic drawings of prominent contemporaries, including his famous sketches of Danton and Marie Antoinette on her way to the guillotine.

David's political career was that of a fervent Jacobin. His earliest activities were particularly concerned with the fate of fellow artists and he worked to abolish the custom whereby the right to exhibit at the Louvre was

22 Robespierre hoped to replace superstitious religious belief with the worship of Reason. In the Festival of Reason, organized by David in November 1793, the goddess of Reason grinds a crucifix under her feet.

confined to a few privileged members of the Royal Academy. At David's instigation, the Assembly voted in August 1791 that the Louvre should be open to all artists without distinction. The Republican press proclaimed: "The chains with which the despotic Academy . . . loaded budding genius . . . have been broken". In the summer of 1792 the Jacobins, led by Marat, proposed David as the "most patriotic and talented of artists" for a seat in the National Convention, where he sat with other members of the Mountain and voted for the King's death in January 1793. He sat on the Committee of General Security and was particularly zealous in persecuting artists who produced royalist propaganda, although it must also be recorded that he protected elderly artists with a royalist past who were no longer a danger to the Republic. His admiration for Marat seems to have been genuine. On one occasion, when Marat was fiercely criticized in the Convention, David rushed to the centre of the hall, bared his chest and shouted impetuously, "Strike here – I demand my own assassination; I, too, am a virtuous man! Liberty will triumph!"

After so complete an identification with the years of terror, it might have been expected that David would suffer either death or disgrace in the aftermath of Thermidor. In fact, he not only survived, but went on to achieve lasting fame as court-painter to Napoleon and recorder of the glories of the Empire. When Robespierre's downfall seemed imminent, David swore "to drink the hemlock" with his idol, but lost his nerve and went into hiding until the crisis had died down. This probably saved his life, for, by the time he was caught, the wave of summary executions was over. David was imprisoned but soon released, and henceforth did all he could to ensure the continuity of his career. Under the Directory he offered, without success, to complete the "Oath of the Tennis Court", substituting the leaders of the Directory for the "insignificant" members of the Assembly originally (but honestly) depicted.

Nicholas Guenot

From his youth, Guenot was employed as a "flotteur", one of the men who floated logs down the rivers to Paris from the forests north and west. It was ill-paid and dangerous work and left Guenot with a grudge against society. A disastrous period of service in the army, from which he was dishonourably discharged for persistent brawling, confirmed his development as a violent and bitter man. With the revolution came his chance to get even

23 The title of this painting speaks for itself: "The Last Roll Call of the Condemned". The figure seated in the centre is reputed to be the poet, André Chenier, arrested by Guenot.

with life. The historian, Richard Cobb, comments:

Guenot is a man to whom the revolution came almost at the right moment, . . . as an opportunity to better himself as well as to escape from a life previously marked by constant failure. (*Reactions to the French Revolution*, O.U.P., 1972)

Cobb might also have added that it gave Guenot an opportunity to pay off old scores. He had connections with the Parisian underworld and was eventually employed by the Committee of General Security as a police spy. In March 1794 he made his mark on history when he arrested the poet André Chenier; but more significant were his denunciations of those who had wronged him in the past, including a group of timber merchants from his home village, who had the misfortune to meet him by chance in a café. When making arrests, he accompanied his activities with blood-curdling threats against the rich.

In spite of his terrorist past, Guenot survived the counter-terror. However, for so undisciplined a character, life in Napoleon's Paris, with its efficient police force, was too uncomfortable, and he returned to his native village in 1800. There he had the misfortune to find one of his former victims installed as mayor. Hounded from the community, Guenot spent the remaining thirty-two years of his life as an outcast in the woods, half mad and a figure of legendary terror to the village children.

The Opponents Of The Revolution

In July 1789 a group of ultra-conservative nobles, denounced by popular orators as leaders of a plot to stifle the reform movement at birth, fled to safety across France's eastern frontiers. They included the King's brother, the Duc d'Artois, and members of the powerful Condé and Polignac families. Although 20,000 passports were issued in the next two months, emigration did not reach its height until 1792. While there was hope that the revolution would not go beyond reform of the grossest social abuses and the establishment of a constitutional monarchy, many aristocrats remained sympathetic. Two such "liberal" nobles, the Duc d'Aiguillon and the Vicomte de Noailles, piloted the first stages of the abolition of feudal dues. Events thereafter threw increasing numbers into exile and opposition. Dumouriez, for example, an ex-royalist general, steadfastly led the Republican armies against the Austrians until April 1793. In that month, outraged by the execution of the King and the political faction-fighting in Paris, and under increasing criticism for the defeat at Neerwinden, he pleaded with his armies to march on Paris and restore the constitution of 1791. When the army refused to co-operate, he defected to the Austrians along with the rest of his general staff. Lafayette, hero of 1789 and first commander of the National Guard, had preceded him in August 1792, only to be imprisoned by the Austrians as a dangerous radical.

Likewise, although refusal to comply with the requirements of the 1790 Civil Constitution of Clergy had placed many priests under suspicion, it was only in 1792, with the threat of foreign invasion and the growth of the dechristianization movement, that life became totally impossible for refractory priests. At that year's Bastille Day celebrations in Bordeaux, for example, a priest was decapitated by the crowd and his head impaled on a stick and carried round the streets. From beyond France's frontiers, the emigrés plotted, in co-operation with foreign governments, for the restoration of the monarchy.

Not all opponents of the revolution were exiled nobles and clergy. As factional disputes developed among the revolutionists, opposition to the current governing group increased. In the summer of 1793, Girondins, driven out of Paris, tried unsuccessfully to set up centres of resistance in Caen and Bordeaux. Robespierre's overthrow was engineered by former colleagues who feared that he was plotting their destruction. Then, with the relaxation of the strict government of the Year II, numerous opportunities arose for revenge, either personal or ideological, against the revolutionary governments of the past five years. This period was known as the "White Terror". In Lyons, for example, the self-styled Company of Jesus assassinated local citizens who had had connections with the Committee of Public Safety, and threw their bodies into the Rhone.

Sometimes, opposition arose from a sense of local pride and a refusal to be dictated to from Paris. The revolt in the Vendée that began in March 1793 was triggered off by the introduction of conscription and requisitioning in an area accustomed to a measure of de facto independence from Paris, and where the influence of the Catholic religion was still strong. When Jacobin-dominated Revolutionary Committees went out from Paris to supervise the revolution in the provinces in March 1793, several large cities, including Lyons, rebelled. In August the citizens of Toulon handed the town over to the British fleet. By July 1794 economic privation had thrown Paris into opposition to Robespierre, for bread prices were now so high that they absorbed over half the daily wage of a semi-skilled craftsman.

Active foreign opposition grew steadily. Urged on by emigrés and by the pleas of Marie Antoinette to her brother, the Austrian Emperor, Austria and Prussia issued the Declaration of Pillnitz in August 1791, which proclaimed the common interest of all the rulers of Europe in restoring the French King to his full power. Revolutionary France reacted to the threat with vigour. In October 1791 Brissot called for armed action to disperse the emigrés, and in April 1792 war was declared on Austria and Prussia. In November, France offered assistance to all foreign peoples fighting for their liberty, and in February 1793 war was declared on Britain. The spectre of revolutionary France surrounded by enemies had become a reality and was to affect profoundly the course of events within France itself.

Madame de la Tour du Pin (1770-1853)

Henrietta-Lucy, who married the Count de la Tour du Pin in 1787, at the age of seventeen, was a member of a fashionable aristocratic circle. Her great-uncle and guardian was the Archbishop of Narbonne; her father's second wife was a cousin of the future Empress Josephine. Shortly after her marriage, Madame de la Tour herself was appointed as a lady-in-waiting to the Queen at Versailles and witnessed, at first-hand, the fate of her class.

As late as the summer of 1789, she little suspected the upheaval that was approaching. On 13 July her groom was sent from Versailles to collect some possessions from her Paris house. Recalling the event some forty years later, Madame comments:

I tell you this very minor circumstance to show you that we had not the slightest presentiment of what was to happen in Paris the next day. All the talk was of a few isolated disturbances at the doors of certain bakers whom the people had accused of adulterating the flour . . . . When you think that I was so situated as to hear all that went on . . . that I went every day to Versailles for supper with Madame de Poix, whose husband was the commander of the guard and saw the King every evening, you will be amazed at what I am about to tell you.

Our feeling of security was so complete that at midday, and even later, on the 14th neither my aunt nor I had any suspicion that there had been the slightest disturbance in Paris.

If anything, Madame de la Tour was more than normally observant, and her political

24 The civilized pleasures of the aristocracy sheltered them from the realities of a crumbling political system. To many, the events of the summer of 1789 came as a complete surprise.

blindness was shared to an even greater degree by her acquaintances. Even the politically-aware among them gravely underestimated the scope of the eruption to come:

Amid all the pleasures, we were drawing near to the month of August, laughing and dancing our way to the precipice. Thinking people were content to talk of abolishing all the abuses. France, they said, was about to be reborn. The word "revolution" was never uttered. Had anyone dared to use it he would have been thought mad. In the upper classes, this illusion of security misled the wise who wanted to see an end to the abuses and to the wasting of public money. This is why so many upright and honourable people, including the King himself who fully shared the illusion, hoped that they were about to enter a golden age . . . . People who frequented my aunt's company and my aunt herself were never short of ideas for reforming abuses and for establishing a fairer distribution of taxes. People were particularly insistent on the need to base the new French constitution on that of England, which few people knew anything about.

The Tour du Pin family soon became convinced opponents of the revolution. One reason for this is described as follows:

25 Many aristocrats fled to safety abroad; others saw this as a cowardly dereliction of duty.

The happenings of the night of 4th August when, on the motion of the Vicomte de Noailles, it was decreed that feudal rights should be abolished, ought to have convinced even the most incredulous that the National Assembly was unlikely to stop at this first measure of dispossession. The decree ruined my father-in-law and our family fortunes never recovered from the effect of that night's session . . . since then we have been forced to contrive a living, sometimes by the sale of some of the few possessions remaining to us, sometimes by taking salaried posts.

They conceived it as their duty to remain by the King and to moderate, as far as possible, the effects of the revolution. They had nothing but contempt for those who emigrated; Madame likened it to "deserting one's post in the face of the enemy".

For a short period in 1789 her father-in-law served as Minister of War:

My father-in-law's distaste for his ministry increased daily. Nearly all the regiments of the army were in a state of revolt. Most of the officers, instead of meeting the efforts of the revolutionaries with firmness, sent in their resignations and left France. To emigrate became a point of honour. Those who remained with their regiments or in their province received letters from emigré officers reproaching them for their cowardice and lack of loyalty to the royal family. Elderly gentlemen who returned to their manors received through the post small parcels containing a white feather or an insulting caricature. It was an attempt to convince them that they had a duty to abandon their sovereign.

By December 1792, however, the Tour du Pins felt under increasing personal threat. They spent a brief period in Holland, and Madame recalled their return to France:

I had scarcely crossed the border when the revolution was all about me, dark and menacing, laden with dangers.

They dared not return to their own house but rented an absent friend's, in the village of

26 The execution of Louis XVI on the Place de la Révolution. The rolling of the drums could be heard at the Tour du Pins' house, outside the walls of Paris.

Passy, near Paris:

It was too big for our household, so we were able to leave all the windows on the street front shut and give the impression that the house was unoccupied. We used the concierge's small entrance. There were two or three other entrances as well which made it a good hiding place . . . an old cabriolet with a fairly broken-down horse, whose real owner I never discovered, used to take us to Paris and we were able to avoid sharing the secret of our hiding-place with all the cab drivers of the city.

The news of the King's execution was a great blow which the Tour du Pins received "in a shocked silence hardly daring to say a word to one another"; they could not believe that "so great a crime would be committed unchallenged". It did, however, relieve them of the moral obligation to remain in France. In 1790 Monsieur de la Tour du Pin had been involved in the suppression of a mutiny at Nancy. In March 1793 his father was arrested and accused by the Paris Commune of causing "the deaths of good patriots". It was obvious that the father had been mistaken for the son, and the family decided to leave Paris for the Girondist stronghold of Bordeaux, from where escape to Spain would be relatively easy. Their plans to leave France altogether were upset, however, by the swift surrender of Bordeaux to the Jacobins. Once more in fear of their lives, the Tour du Pins witnessed daily executions of the opponents of the Jacobins. Madame recalled:

The guillotine was set up permanently in the Place Dauphine. The small group of fanatics who escorted it met with no opposition when they brought it into Bordeaux, though a few cannon shots fired into their close ranks would certainly have put them to flight. But the people of Bordeaux, who, only the previous day, had been declaring with true Gascon flourish their intention to resist, did not even show themselves in the deserted streets. The boldest shut their shops, the young men hid or fled and by evening terror reigned in the city. So great was this terror that when an order was published directing every holder of arms, under pain of death, to take them before midday the next day to the lawns of La Trompette, barrows could be seen passing along the streets and people furtively throwing into them every weapon they possessed. It was noticed that some of these probably had not been used for at least two generations.

As Madame de la Tour was eight months pregnant, escape for the whole family was impossible, but her husband was forced to flee from the town in dramatic circumstances:

While all this was going on, I gave birth to a daughter whom I named Seraphine, after her father, who stayed just long enough to give her his blessing. At the moment of the birth we learned of the arrest of many people in neighbouring houses. My doctor's maidservant came out from the town to tell him that they were looking for him in order to arrest him and that seals had been put on his house. That night we placed a trustworthy gentlewoman on the road leading to Canoles, telling her to give us warning of any sound of people approaching so that, if danger threatened, my husband and the doctor would be able to escape through the vineyards.

Within twenty-four hours Monsieur de la Tour had need of this escape route and spent the next few months in a series of improvised hiding places. He first turned to:

a former groom of his father's, a man whom he trusted completely and who belonged to the district. This man kept a small inn and he offered to hide my husband, but he had young children and was afraid they might unwittingly betray him. He therefore suggested that it would be much safer to seek refuge with his brother-in-law, a good well-to-do locksmith named Potier, who was married but childless. This man was quite willing to shelter my husband, though for a handsome consideration, and, the deal being concluded, he put him in a safe place in his house, in a small windowless room leading off the bedroom.

Years later Madame visited this hiding place and thought it a "dreadful hole". It was separated by only:

a thin plank from the shop where the boys worked and where the forge and bellows were installed. When the locksmith and his wife left the room, always taking the key with them, my husband had to lie quite still on his bed in order not to make the slightest noise. He was also strongly urged not to have any light, in case it was seen from the workshop.

Meanwhile, Madame stayed in Bordeaux, making every effort to keep her identity secret. As food could only be bought by those in possession of a ration card, for which each person had to declare himself, it required considerable ingenuity to maintain anonymity:

... an order was issued that a notice should be posted up at the entrance to every house giving the names of all the people living there .... The orders were printed on paper with a tricolour edging and at the top was written, "Liberty, Equality, Fraternity or Death". Everyone tried to fill in the required declaration as illegibly as possible. Ours was written in an excessively fine hand and placed up very high so that it was difficult to read. Many were written in an ink so pale that the first rain made the names illegible .... The section bread was made of all types of flour, was black and tacky, and people today would hesitate to give it to their dogs. It was delivered straight from the ovens and people stood in queues ... to buy it. It is a very odd fact that people found a kind of pleasure in these gatherings. The terror in which we lived prevented us from exchanging more than a word or two when we met, and the queues represented, as it were, a lawful assembly where the timid could talk to their neighbours and learn the latest news.

In December 1793 M. Potier witnessed the execution of a man who had sheltered a nobleman, and felt unable to hide M. de la Tour any longer. Madame decided that they must leave France altogether and concocted some fantastic plans, none of which were carried out. One was that:

he [an Italian friend called Ferrari] and I should take a passport to Toulouse, with my husband as our servant. I was to pass as his widowed daughter, taking her children back to Italy to her husband's family. In the main cities along our route, such as Marseilles and Toulouse, we would give concerts. I sang sufficiently well to pass as a singer without my ability being questioned. Every day we practised different pieces which we planned to offer.

In March 1794 the Tour du Pin family finally escaped on an American ship, the *Diana*, bound for Boston. The boarding was so furtive that the emigrants dared not be seen buying provisions. Consequently, they started the voyage with only "a few jars of potted goose, a few sacks of potatoes and French beans, a small case of bottled jam and fifty bottles of Bordeaux".

After an adventurous exile in the United States and England, the Tour du Pins returned to France under Napoleon's government. Forced to earn his living, Monsieur served as prefect in Brussels between 1801 and 1812. He resumed his diplomatic career after the Restoration and was one of the ambassadors plenipotentiary for France at the Congress of Vienna. He remained loyal to the Bourbons and went into exile with Charles X in 1830. He died in 1837, but Madame de la Tour survived until 1853, outliving all but one of her six children. Looking back on her experiences, she realized that the months of danger had profoundly changed her character:

Looking critically at my past life I reproached myself for its futility. Some presentiment of other fates in store made me resolve very firmly to put away for ever the thought of carefree youth, the far from disinterested flatteries of this world and the small successes to which I had aspired.

François-René de Chateaubriand (1768-1848)

During his long life Chateaubriand managed to be at odds with almost every regime under which he lived. He claimed to have:

met nearly all the men who in my time have played a part in my own and their country's histories, from Washington to Napoleon, from Louis XVIII to Alexander I, from Pius VII to Gregory XVI, from Fox to Burke ... to Mirabeau, from Nelson, Bolivar and Mehemet Ali, to Suffren and Bougainville [famous French admirals]
(Memoirs of Chateaubriand)

He was to become Foreign Minister of France under Louis XVIII (1814-24), "taking my place, as a minister and ambassador, trimmed with gold lace and plastered with ribbons and decorations, at the table of kings". But before that, he had lived in the wigwams of the Huron Indians, wearing "the bearskin cloak of the savages", and subsisted in the direst poverty as an exile in London.

Chateaubriand's achievements were remarkable and his memoirs have been accepted as an important work of literature; yet he was unable to find lasting satisfaction in

27 Chateaubriand – star-crossed member of the old aristocracy of France.

anything he did. As a young man, he had hunted with Louis XVI and had been given the chance to gain the King's favour. But:

Society struck me as even more odious than I had imagined it.... I took an invincible dislike to the Court and at the moment of triumph and favour I jumped into my carriage and returned to Paris.

He welcomed the idea of social and political reform but was sickened by the reality of revolution. On one occasion he saw:

two dishevelled and disfigured heads ... each at the end of a pike. The murderers stopped in front of me and stretched the pikes up ... to bring the pale effigies closer to my face. One eye in one of these heads had started from its socket and was hanging down on the dead man's face.

The vision of these and other heads made Chateaubriand resolve to leave France. His destination was clear, for

one idea obsessed me, the idea of going to the United States. I proposed to discover the North-West Passage [the supposed route to China via the top of North America].

Accordingly, in 1791, he sailed from St Malo to Chesapeake Bay. There he met Washington, but had insufficient funds to set up the exploratory expedition of which he dreamed. Staying in a farmhouse in the wilderness of Tennessee, he came across a newspaper with the headline "Flight of the King", describing the capture of Louis and Marie Antoinette at Varennes. Remembering his roots as a soldier and a nobleman, Chateaubriand told himself, "So back to France!", and by December 1791 was en route for Le Havre, to serve in the royalist army being mustered by emigrés in Belgium. He took his time over the journey, married an heiress on the way (who turned out not to have the expected fortune), and arrived in Lille in August 1792, the latter part of the journey being conducted through northern France, in fear of exposure and arrest. There were as

28 Chateaubriand's enthusiasm for the revolution was shattered by the gruesome reality of 14 July 1789, when the heads of Flesselles and de Launay were paraded through the streets of Paris.

many divisions in emigré circles as there were among Republicans, and Chateaubriand's reception was lukewarm. He was told:

You ought to have been here three years ago, you're one of those people who wait to see how things will turn out before they make up their minds. You've arrived when victory is certain; we've no use for you.

Eventually, however, the influence of friends gained acceptance for Chateaubriand. He found the emigrés a motley crew; thrown together by chance, they included whole families – fathers and sons, nephews and uncles, brothers and cousins – ranging in age from teenagers to grandfathers. Chateaubriand encountered the elderly father of a friend killed at the beginning of the revolution, who was splashing barefoot through the mud, with his shoes slung from his bayonet to save wear.

Optimistic predictions about the certainty of victory proved to be totally unfounded. The emigré brigades, too few and disorganized to fight alone, were under the overall command of the Duke of Brunswick, the Prussian commander. The Prussian army was severely hit by dysentery, partly caused by the appallingly wet autumn of 1792, and Brunswick was therefore reluctant to risk the loss of even more troops in open battle. Repulsed on the first day of the Battle of Valmy, he refused to renew the attack, in spite of the pleas of the Duc d'Artois; he told the poet, Goethe, who was present as an observer, "You will bear witness that I have been defeated by the elements". In the retreat that followed, Chateaubriand was brought near to death by a septic leg wound, dysentery and smallpox. On one particularly bad day, he lay down in the mud and begged his comrades to leave him, for "I'd rather die". He survived to reach Jersey, where friends nursed him back to health.

Chateaubriand's next ambition was to join the rebels in the Vendée. From this he was dissuaded by Pierre de Bouillon, leader of the 3,000 French emigrés on Jersey, who told him, "You are in no state to live in caves and forests". Bouillon advised a move to England where, since war had been declared on Republican France on 1 February, an emigré army had been in formation. Chateaubriand recalled his arrival in May 1793:

I disembarked at Southampton, an obscure and humble traveller.

His passport described him as:

François de Chateaubriand, French officer in the emigrant army, five feet four inches high, thin-shapen, brown hair and pitted with the smallpox.

He shared a carriage to London with some sailors on leave, and took lodgings in a garret off the Tottenham Court Road. There he descended into poverty:

I was consumed with hunger: I burst with fever; sleep had deserted me; I sucked pieces of linen which I had soaked in water: I chewed grass and paper.... On one bitter winter's night I stood for two hours outside a shop that sold dried fruit.... I could have eaten not only the foodstuffs, but the boxes and baskets in which they were packed.

A gift of forty Crowns from his uncle saved Chateaubriand, but he could see no future "but the workhouse or the Thames". Eventually, however, he swallowed his aristocratic pride and took paid employment as a translator of twelfth-century French manuscripts. In his spare time he wrote *Essai sur les Revolutions*, which appeared in 1797 and made his name in French emigré circles in London. During this time Chateaubriand heard of the execution or death in prison of one member of his family after another.

His exile ended when Napoleon became First Consul and "restored order by despotism". Chateaubriand's troubles, however, were by no means over; he was fêted, then exiled, by both Napoleon and Louis XVIII. Perhaps, though, his moment of triumph came when he returned to England as French ambassador in 1822. This time he embarked for London with a passport worded:

Give passage to His Lordship the Vicomte de Chateaubriand, Peer of France, Ambassador of the King to His Britannic Majesty.

Baron de Batz (1761-1822)

Baron Jean de Batz was something of an exception amongst aristocratic emigrés, in that he returned to France in 1792 and worked to undermine the revolution from within.

Little is known of his early life, but a note written by his commanding officer indicates that in his youth he was something of a feckless playboy aristocrat:

17 September 1784
I never saw M. de Batz with his regiment, and Monseigneur had given me instructions to imprison him, if he should ever come.

He represented the First Estate of his native Gascony in the Estates General, where he spoke rarely and gave few indications of his opinions. Having emigrated early in 1792, he returned to Paris at the end of the year and lodged with Mademoiselle Grandmaison, an actress, who later became his mistress. He sold his own house on the outskirts of Paris to her brother, for a nominal sum, and continued to use it as a hideout.

Involved in a plot to rescue the King on his way to the guillotine, Batz masterminded a similarly abortive scheme to free Marie Antoinette from the Temple. A police report of February 1793 reveals what the authorities knew about the latter plot:

Batz was to have been admitted . . . with thirty men who meant to make their fortune out of it and were already well-paid. They were to guard the turret with the staircase in it. Michonis, who was in league with Batz, had had himself posted upstairs. At midnight the sentries were to be Batz's men, and the royal family were to leave their rooms after the three doors on the staircase were in the hands of their friends. If necessary anyone who opposed them was to be killed, and the royal family were to go out with the patrol, disguised in greatcoats.

From this point onwards, it becomes difficult to be certain about the exact extent of Batz's activities. In 1793-94 a series of financial scandals occurred, involving leading Republicans, which contributed to the splits in the revolutionary movement and helped to convince Robespierre that his rivals were untrustworthy and unpatriotic. In November 1793 one of the implicated politicians, Chabot, wrote in his diary:

I have denounced a system of corruption intended to disgrace the members of the National Convention . . . and I have been in solitary confinement for two months, while,

29 Baron de Batz – royalist conspirator.

perhaps, the heads of the conspiracy are carrying out their infernal plot.

When I denounced the former Baron de Batz I ought to have expected this subversion of the principles of justice. His only object in remaining in France was to act as the most energetic agent of the emigrants.

Two warrants were issued for Batz's arrest; the second, in April 1794, read:

The Committee [of General Security] enjoins upon you to redouble your efforts to discover the infamous Batz. Remember that his agents are everywhere, even in the prisons. . . . . tell everyone that he is outlawed, and has a price upon his head; that a description of him is published everywhere and he cannot escape; that everything must be discovered and that there will be no mercy for those who could have given him up and did not do so.

There is little doubt that Batz played an influential role in undermining Republican solidarity, but there is equally little doubt that Robespierre exaggerated the influence of one man and used him as a scapegoat to explain, probably quite sincerely, the growth of opposition to his government. An unconvincing attempt was made to link Batz with Cecile Renault (page 46), and on 17 June 1794 Mlle Grandmaison and her servant Nicole were tried with her.

Batz himself was never caught and remained in Paris to become involved in the royalist rising of 13 Vendémiaire, which first brought Napoleon Bonaparte to prominence. An eye-witness reported one incident:

Indeed such was the confusion that reigned in this general's head [commander of the pro-royalist Parisians] that he had omitted to put anyone in command of the Peletier column, though the others were to follow it! M. de Batz, having observed a young officer, M. Chartier, who was disposing his men admirably and seemed to have the gift of encouraging them in words very much to the point, said to him: "Young man, take command of the whole column resolutely, and they will all obey you." Chartier took command and was obeyed.
column resolutely, and they will all obey you." Chartier took command and was obeyed.

From 1795 to 1815 Batz's career fades into obscurity. On Louis XVIII's accession, a commission of emigrés and retired army officers was set up to examine the credentials of royalists asking for posts under the new regime. After listing Batz's services to the Crown, the report on him continued:

The Commission . . . begs his Excellency the Minister of War to call to His Majesty's attention the services of this field-officer, who deserves some special mark of distinction for his devotion,

30 Enemies of the Republic like de Batz gained great satisfaction from the capacity of the revolutionaries for destroying each other. Here, Chabot, whom de Batz claims to have incriminated, stands trial with Danton and Desmoulins before the Revolutionary Tribunal.

zeal and great qualities, of which he has given abundant proof.

At the restoration of 1815 his promotion to the rank of field-marshal was confirmed, and in 1816 he was given command of the Department of the Cantal. From the fragmented record of his life little definitive can be discovered about Batz's personality, but his behaviour after the Bourbon restoration would indicate that he was motivated throughout by a deep-seated sense of aristocratic superiority and contempt for the common people. Until he died in 1822 he treated the local peasants with such brutality that, in revenge, they nicknamed him "the robber".

Charlotte Corday (1768-93)

Marie-Charlotte de Corday d'Armont was born into a Norman family of untainted noble blood, who could trace their lineage back to 1077. Her father, however, was a third son, whose share of the family lands was small and who could afford so little hired help that he often ploughed his own fields. He became increasingly bitter at the social conventions that forced him to maintain the status of a gentleman on a poor farmer's income (he scrimped and scraped to send his sons to an exclusive military academy), and his children grew up in a home where the Ancien Régime and the feudal system were often criticized and Rousseau was read.

Charlotte's uncle, who supervised her education, introduced her early to classical history, the fashionable subject of study in late eighteenth-century France. During her isolated childhood, the men of ancient Rome and Sparta became her heroes and she dreamed of the rebirth of France through the sacrifices of great and noble men. Once she wrote in despair:

> O great Republics! Full of austere virtues and heroic action! Your like will not be seen in our age. Frenchmen are not pure enough, not generous-hearted enough, to understand or copy you. O frivolous nation, you need to be regenerated and to base your national life on the ancient traditions of beauty, greatness, truth and nobility.

Like other impractical romantics, Charlotte saw the revolution as the dawn of a new era of liberty and justice. While her brothers joined the emigré army in Germany, Charlotte adopted the Girondins as the heroes who would regenerate France. A guest at a dinner which Charlotte also attended has left a description of her at this time. Always a pretty girl, she had become positively radiant with enthusiasm:

> Mlle. de Corday, wearing a dress made of one of those beautiful materials given to her by an old relative, was a dazzling spectacle.... I can still see her clad in an over-dress of pink taffeta, with white stripes, opening on an underskirt of white silk. Her costume showed off her figure to perfection.... She looked more animated than usual.

At the same dinner, Charlotte scandalized the guests by refusing to drink the King's health.

However, her romantic nature ill-equipped her to live with the violent reality of revolution. As Jacobin influence spread to Caen, where she lodged with her aunt, she wrote to a friend of her "contempt for life, disdain of any existence without purpose, the complete disenchantment of a spirit that finds itself deceived after having cherished long and delicious illusions". She despised the King but found his execution sickening. In May 1793 proscribed Girondins, fleeing from Paris, arrived in Caen and issued a proclamation urging people to march on Paris and "set up again the brilliant statue of liberty". Seeing the men she admired defeated and outlawed, Charlotte resolved to emulate the heroes of old and eliminate, singlehanded, the man she held most responsible for the sullying of the revolution – the Jacobin agitator, Jean-Paul Marat. On 6 July 1793 she booked a seat on the Paris coach, bought a pair of stout shoes suitable for the capital and wrote a note to her father telling him she was leaving for England. In Paris, on the morning of 13 July, she purchased a sharp kitchen knife, which she concealed in her bodice. That evening she bluffed her way into Marat's lodging. He suffered from a painful skin complaint and was soaking in a medicinal bath. A board rested on his knees, which he used as a desk; he was editing the next copy of his inflammatory paper, *The People's Friend*. Charlotte thrust the knife vigorously into Marat's chest, passing through the lung and piercing the aorta. He gave a hoarse cry and died. Charlotte was immediately apprehended by Laurent Bas, who was folding copies of *The People's Friend* in Marat's office. In the following testimony Bas refers to himself in the third person:

> Citizen Bas seeing the assassin coming towards him took up a chair in order to stop her. The monster, by a great effort, had succeeded in reaching the anteroom, when Bas gave her a blow with the chair which stretched her on the ground. She got up at once and looked significantly at the window of the anteroom, which opened on to the courtyard. Bas seized her by the breasts, threw her down and struck her.

Charlotte Corday had intended to be caught; she carried with her not only her birth certificate, but also an "Address to the French People" explaining her motives:

31 Charlotte Corday – disillusioned romantic.

32 David's idealized portrait of the dead Marat was the tribute of one ardent revolutionary to another.

When Marat, vilest of scoundrels, whose name stands for numberless crimes, falls under the avenging knife, the Mountain will tremble. Danton and Robespierre will pale, and all the other brigands seated on their bloody thrones will shiver before the thunder that the gods, avengers of humanity, only suspend in order to make their final downpour more awful.

She gaily courted a martyr's death and immortality. In prison, she begged the authorities to have her portrait painted for posterity. Her trial was a formality; the verdict and sentence were never in doubt. Serene to the end, she was able to joke as the red gown of an assassin was pulled over her head: "Here is a death toilette made by hands a little rude, but it will lead to immortality". Her execution was witnessed by Forster, a German Rhinelander drawn to Paris by his admiration for the early stage of the revolution. He recalled:

She looked with an expression of indescribable sweetness at the ebb and flow of the multitude and when the populace, mad with excitement, or a group of furies disguised as women hailed her with strident cries, a glance from her beautiful eyes was sufficient to reduce them to silence.

As her testament shows, Charlotte's serenity stemmed from her conviction that she had saved France; there were others, equally naive, who shared this belief. Forster wrote to his wife that it was obvious that Charlotte had loved "liberty and the Republic with enthusiasm" and her memory would live on in the "hearts of those who admire simple goodness". Petion, one of the Caen Girondins, wrote shortly before his death:

In ordinary times justice alone should strike the guilty. But in the present conditions the murder of Marat is an act of national justice. A woman has set an example to men! May they profit by the lesson and purge France of the scoundrels who are oppressing her.

Their judgement was wildly wrong. Marat's assassination provided a further justification for the Jacobin terror, for, in the words of one deputy, it was obvious that Paris in the summer of 1793 was full of Charlotte Cordays, "monsters foaming with rage, who are only waiting for the favourable moment to fall on patriots and cut their throats". Within months, the Committee of Public Safety was supreme in Paris, the Girondins were scattered and Marat had been converted into a popular saint whose bust was carried through the streets with religious fervour and after whom children were named.

Raoul Hesdin

Raoul Hesdin, a Frenchman by birth, lived for some months in Paris as a spy in the pay of the British government. All that is known of his life and opinions must be gleaned from a private diary he kept between December 1793 and July 1794. From this record it emerges that Hesdin had been familiar with the French capital under the Ancien Régime and in the early days of the revolution. After exile in England and the United States, he returned to France with forged papers and was employed as an official engraver by the Committee of Public Safety. Obviously a man of some education, he belonged to that class of skilled craftsmen that provided so many recruits for the sans-culottes movement; as such, he was able to pose convincingly as a fervent Jacobin and mix intimately with members of the Convention and the Paris sections. The information he thus gathered was forwarded to London. Although Hesdin was a biased observer and depicted the revolutionaries of 1793-94 in the worst possible light, his diary presents a fascinating picture of Paris under the Committee of Public Safety, and one man's reaction to it.

During the winter of 1793-94 Paris was in the grip of a food shortage, caused partly by the imposition of the Maximum. On 6 January Hesdin recorded:

Famine, famine! When the Municipals [City Council] think it necessary, as they did last week, to placard the streets with the joyful tidings that a thousand loaves of sugar have been received by them for distribution to the grocers, we cannot be said to be many days removed from famine.

Bread was rationed and had to be queued for; his landlord's daughters, for example, "who take it in turns to go, are often waiting from four of the clock after midnight till eight or nine in the morning". Things were so bad that, in March, an edict was issued against cultivating gardens for "luxury" and ordering parks to be converted into gardens for growing peas and beans. Hesdin made a comment that throws interesting light on the government's unpopularity among the common people of Paris by the summer of 1794:

We who are not obliged to form queues at the bakers' doors — thanks to my employ, I am exempt from this, and a bare sufficiency of bread is delivered, together with meat and vegetables, at my lodgings daily — have very little conception of the suffering of those who are.

Hesdin was struck by the atmosphere of suspicion that prevailed in Paris:

I often wonder if people outside France are aware of the utter disappearance of gaiety which has accompanied the revolution. The Fete of the tenth day, which has replaced Sunday, is ten times more gloomy than a Sabbath under Cromwell would have been . . . . I speak now not only of the days of the old monarchy but even of '89 and '90. The ferment of minds in the clubs and coffee houses, above all in the streets, was indescribable. People lived literally in the open air those two summers. Now it is the silence of the grave. I was passing down the Rue des Lanternes at nine of the clock yesterday evening; there was a small group talking outside a grocer's booth at the corner of the Marmousets, not more than five people, but a patrol approaching, they all dispersed hurriedly, not a figure in sight for the whole street's length.

Even the arts were government-controlled — a development that, in Hesdin's opinion, led to a marked decline in quality. One evening he watched a new "Republican" drama on the fall of Toulon, that would have been "hissed off the stage" if it had been performed anywhere

33 Early enthusiasm for the revolution among the English was soon replaced by horror, and the reports of spies such as Hesdin fed the determination of the British government to overthrow the young Republic before its subversive doctrines could spread abroad. In this English cartoon (it was assumed that educated readers would understand French), Republican Paris is seen as the destroyer of humanity, religion, law and order, peace, prosperity and domestic tranquillity.

in England. In keeping with the belief that revolutionary France was Ancient Rome reborn:

even when Greek and Roman subjects are represented, the heathen gods are made to speak the language of the "Heroes of the Bastille". . . and the goddesses descend from the wings in tricolour scarves and drawers.

As a Frenchman, Hesdin could not remain emotionally uninvolved; he became increasingly depressed. As early as February 1794 he brooded:

If there were the least chance of my obtaining employment elsewhere or a passport to leave, I would leave this hideous shambles tomorrow.

His mood was even blacker after Danton's execution in April:

Tonight I felt sick and weary of life and wished to God my head was in the basket. The very paving stones smell of blood, and the river seems to run blood. Not a group of chatterers tonight, but there were two or three government agents listening for the least sign of sympathy with an accused person.

In June, Hesdin gloomily estimated the toll of the dead:

It is impossible to arrive at the actual numbers of those in prison, nor have I kept a regular list of the condemned; but to the best of my recollection, over two thousand five hundred persons have perished at the scaffold since the beginning of this year; and to show the fearful rate of the accelerated figures of the bloodshed, eight hundred of these during the last four weeks.

The only hope for a change of government lay in the fact that Robespierre had alienated everyone, even his closest supporters, for he had convinced himself that:

All talent, all eloquence, all fortune, all intelligence, which will not subserve itself to him, is to be destroyed and swept from his path. Suspicion of everyone and everything is his only active principle. His own colleagues in the Committee must live in dread of him.

Hesdin, however, had little real hope that Robespierre would be ousted in the near future, and by 12 July his depression had reached new depths:

Politics seem to be asleep and all hope of resistance at an end; the bloodshed seems perpetual if men can be born fast enough to fuel the fire; Saint-Just more firmly seated than ever; Carnot reduced to silence; Billaud completely at one with Robespierre; the Police Committee and the Nantese [Fouché] trembling for their heads.

This was one of the last entries in the diary. A week later Hesdin's pessimistic forecast was proved wrong when Robespierre was overthrown by a conspiracy amongst his erstwhile colleagues and the Reign of Terror drew to a close.

The Victims Of The Revolution

To the popular imagination, fed on Dickens' *A Tale of Two Cities*, the most numerous victims – massacred in the prisons or dispatched to public execution on the guillotine – came from the class most closely associated with the Ancien Régime: the royal family, the aristocrats and prominent public officials. This is a far from balanced picture.

Although the earliest victims were unpopular royal servants such as de Launay, governor of the Bastille, and de Freneilly, Mayor of Paris, the majority of endangered aristocrats fled to safety abroad. Others, less compromised or more flexible, fitted in with the new governments. Foremost among the latter group was Louis XVI's cousin, Louis Philippe of Orleans, who, as Citizen Egalité, became a member of the Convention and voted for the King's death. Louis himself survived as a puppet king for three years and his actual execution was delayed until 1793. Only from mid-1792 onwards did life become increasingly intolerable for those with associations with the old regime and compromise between aristocracy and revolution become completely impossible. Even flexible Philippe Egalité was condemned to death in September 1793. Those who escaped execution often suffered in other ways. A historian who has examined police records for the Year II has revealed cases of elderly aristocratic ladies, abandoned by their children who had emigrated, throwing themselves out of high windows, having first left a note to the local police chief begging him to care for a lap-dog or a canary.

Throughout the course of the revolution, however, the majority of victims came from the non-aristocratic classes. Of the estimated 1,100 dead in the September 1792 massacres, approximately 365 were political prisoners and between 67% and 72% were ordinary criminals. At the height of the Terror, 85% of those executed after trial belonged to the Third Estate. A series of rapid political changes between 1791 and 1795 meant that yesterday's leaders tended to become tomorrow's victims. Robespierre, virtual dictator for a year, was condemned by his rivals, as he himself had once disposed of Girondins, Hébertists and Dantonists.

Terror reached its height in the spring and summer of 1794, because the Committee of Public Safety saw itself as the embodiment of the will of the people. Criticism, therefore, could never be attributed to an honest difference of opinion between loyal Republicans; it must be the result of treason and a betrayal of the sovereign people. To those who complained in September 1793 that the Committee was becoming too tyrannical, Robespierre replied:

> Whoever seeks to debase, divide or paralyse the Convention, is an enemy of our country, whether he sits in this hall or is a foreigner. Whether he acts from perversity or stupidity, he is of the party of tyrants who make war upon us.

Moreover, if "the people is everywhere good", individual dissidents were unlikely to be acting on their own initiative but rather at the instigation of emigrés and their foreign paymasters. When Jacques Roux, the Parisian demagogue, denounced the June 1793 Constitution for paying insufficient attention to the material needs of the people, Robespierre rounded on him:

> Do you think that this priest, who in concert with the Austrians denounces the best patriots, can have pure views or legitimate intentions?

In such an atmosphere of suspicion, few were safe; and life became even more precarious after the passing of the Law of Suspects in September 1793, which included among the "suspects" the sweeping category of "those who, by their conduct, relations or language spoken or written, have shown themselves partisans of tyranny or federalism and enemies of liberty".

Although the best-documented examples are provided by Paris, it must not be overlooked that the majority of victims died unrecorded in the provinces. It is estimated by one historian that of the 4,554 death sentences passed by revolutionary courts between July and December 1793, over 3,300 occurred in Lyons and the Vendée in December of that year. The massacres in Nantes in November 1793 are discussed on pages 18-20.

Louis Philippe, Duke of Orleans (1747-93)

Descendants of Louis XIV's younger brother, the Orleans family were the second most noble and wealthy family in France, with an annual income of over 800,000 livres. Traditionally, the Bourbon monarchs had feared the ambitions of their Orleans cousins and excluded them from any significant voice in the government of France. They made no exception of Louis Philippe, who succeeded to his father's title in 1787; he had expressed his frustration as early as 1772:

Am I to be condemned to eternal idleness? Even if war should come, what could I hope to do? I am twenty five years old and I have not seen service yet. The navy is my only resource – it is the only post I could take to acquire public esteem and consideration, without which our birthright only puts us lower than others.

He particularly resented Queen Marie Antoinette, believing – with some justification – that many of the slights he received were at her instigation.

In these circumstances it was perhaps inevitable that Louis Philippe should consort with critics of the government. In the 1780s the grounds of his Paris home, the Palais Royale, became a meeting place for dissidents,

34 Louis Philippe in the costume of a Prince of the Blood.

and by 1789 the Orleans family were popular heroes. Madame de la Tour du Pin noted that the people of Paris were prejudiced in their favour:

In the early spring of 1789, after a terrible winter which caused much suffering among the poor, the Duc d'Orleans was extremely popular in Paris. The previous year he had sold many paintings from the fine collection in the palace and it was generally believed that the eight million raised by this sale had been devoted to relieving the sufferings of the people during the hard winter that had just ended. In contrast, whether rightly or wrongly, there was no mention of any charitable gifts from the royal princes or the King and Queen.

In the early months of the revolution, Louis Philippe was in the forefront of the opposition. In the Estates General he headed the group of liberal nobles who united with the Third Estate. His agents had a hand in the Reveillon riots of May 1789; and although he denied it, several eye-witnesses saw the Duke of Orleans among the ring-leaders at Versailles in October 1789. Madame de la Tour du Pin's maid, Marguerite, was there, and Madame recorded what happened:

As she passed the gate in the Rue de l'Orangerie, she had also seen a gentleman arriving, his boots splashed with mud and a riding whip still in his hand. It was none other than the Duc d'Orleans, whom she knew very well by sight. She told us also that, at the sight of him, the wretches had cried joyfully: Long Live our King d'Orleans".

That his popularity in Paris reached new heights at this time is confirmed by the British ambassador, the Duke of Dorset:

The Duke of Orleans has experienced repeated marks of popularity recently and particularly on Tuesday last. As he was returning through the Faubourg St Antoine the people frequently called out "Vive la maison d'Orleans". (October 1789)

Yet the Duke was neither a skilled nor a principled political leader. His motives were purely personal. He told Brissot in 1790:

Do not imagine that I made this stand against the King in order to serve a people I despise . . . only that I was indignant at them [the royal family] treating me with so much violence.

On several occasions he showed a willingness to abandon his revolutionary colleagues, in return for royal favour. In August 1789 he told his English friend, Grace Elliot, that:

The King and Queen disliked him and that they would endeavour to poison him; that although he wished ever to be of much use to the King and Queen, they would never believe him to be sincere . . . he thought himself very cruelly used, as he really meant to be of use to the King. (*Grace Elliot, Journal of My Life during the French Revolution,* 1859)

Mirabeau, for one, could never regard him as a serious or dangerous politician, advising the King:

The Duke is despised and incapable. What is there to fear from such a man? . . . Let him be well received at court. The mark of the King's goodness will enchain him and his peace with the Court will prevent the Jacobins from claiming him. The fear of losing his domains in a complete upheaval will restrain him. (July 1790)

It was only when the royal family made it quite clear that they distrusted him totally that Louis Philippe decided to "make friends of his own" and finally threw in his lot with the Jacobins later that year. His eldest son, the Duke of Chartres and future King Louis Philippe, even joined the Jacobin Club and the Republican Army.

Once the break had been made with his class and background, there was no turning back; yet the Duke felt increasingly that he was at the mercy of events beyond his control and men cleverer and more unscrupulous than himself. Grace Elliot remembered his mood in the summer of 1792:

The Duke came to dine twice with me in the country, and I found his manner much altered. He was low-spirited, which never was his natural character.

He would have liked to opt out of politics completely. He told Grace that he had always:

envied the life of an English country gentleman; and though his enemies taxed him with wanting to be King, he would willingly change his lot and all his fortune for a small estate in England.

He quarrelled with his wife, who heartily disapproved of their son's association with the Jacobin Club, and they became completely estranged.

In January 1793 the Duke of Orleans committed the two acts for which history best remembers him. He abandoned his aristocratic titles, adopting the family name "Egalité" (Equality), and, in the National Convention, he voted in favour of the King's death. His long-standing bitterness against the royal family played a part in his decision, but the strongest motive was probably the knowledge that his own fate, and that of his family, depended on constant proof of his loyalty to the Jacobin cause. He told Grace Elliot despairingly:

You cannot, must not, judge me. I know my own situation. I could not avoid doing what I have done, I am perhaps more to be pitied than you can form an idea of. I am more a slave of faction than anyone in France.

It was not enough. Ostracized by his own class, Louis Philippe remained suspect to the revolutionaries. At four in the morning on 14 April 1793 he was arrested in bed at the Palais Royale (now the Palais Egalité). After six months' imprisonment in Marseilles and Paris, he was tried and condemned as a traitor. The removal of responsibility seems to have given Louis Philippe peace of mind. The commissioners who escorted him and his fellow prisoners to Marseilles reported to the Committee of Public Safety:

The Citizen Conti, because of his age and his infirmities, feels the bitterness of his position very deeply. As for Citizen Egalité, he shows more resolution than the others and appears to find in the company of his children weapons against the boredom and sadness of his solitude.

He died with more dignity than he had lived. Grace Elliot received a full report of the execution from her servant, who was present:

He looked, my servant told me, as he did in former days when he was going out on any occasion of ceremony. He was very much powdered and looked very well. His hands were tied behind him and his coat thrown over his shoulders . . . . When the cart moved from the Palais Royale the Duke looked at the mob with a sort of indignation. He did not alter in any way, but carried his head high till the cart turned on to the Place Louis XV; then he saw the scaffold before him; my man said that he turned very pale but still held up his head . . . he leaped up the ladder with great haste, looked around at everybody, helped the executioner undo his neckcloth and did not speak one word or make the least resistance.

Even his critic, Beaulieu, an eye-witness, acknowledged that:

The Duke of Orleans, who until then had not passed for a courageous man, showed,

35 Contemporaries believed that the fateful march of the women to Versailles and the forceable return of the King to Paris were instigated by the Duke of Orleans. This has never been conclusively proved.

however, the greatest fortitude in his last moments ... he appeared at the moment of his trial to have found again the character that a Frenchman likes to find in a descendant of Henry IV.

Among historians, Louis Philippe's reputation is almost uniformly bad. He is depicted as a man so ambitious for the Crown that he was willing to connive even in the death of his cousin. There is some truth in this picture. Yet Louis Philippe was neither ruthless nor unscrupulous enough to be a real villain, and soon found himself the victim of men shrewder than himself. In the end, the certainty of death seemed preferable to the uncertainties of a volatile political situation.

The Renault Family

In 1794 the Renault household consisted of Antoine, a self-employed stationery merchant; his thirty-one year-old son, Jacques, who helped in the business and was therefore exempt from compulsory military service; twenty year-old Cecile; and an elderly aunt, who had been a nun until the dissolution of her convent two years earlier. Members of the family who no longer lived at home included two younger sons serving with the Republican Army, and a married daughter. The first four became public celebrities for a brief period in the summer of 1794. They left no written testimony of their own and little is known of their lives and opinions before 24 May 1794; yet, from records of their interrogation before the Revolutionary Tribunal, it is clear that at least some members of the Renault family were innocent victims of the current atmosphere of hysteria and suspicion.

On the evening of 24 May Cecile Renault stole from home. On 26 May Barère, for the Committee of Public Safety, gave the Convention the following account of her subsequent activities:

At nine o'clock in the evening, a young girl appeared at the Duplay house [where Robespierre lodged] and demanded to see Robespierre. The eldest Duplay daughter answered that he had gone out. At that the girl replied with a show of temper that "he was a public official and that it was his business to see everyone who comes".

That irreverent language caused her to be arrested and brought before the Committee of General Security. On the way she said to those who had arrested her, "Under the old regime, when people went to see the King, they were admitted at once." "So you regret the days when there was a king?" She replied, "Ah, I would give the last drop of my blood to have one. In my

36 This contemporary engraving shows the arrest of Cecile Renault outside Robespierre's lodging.

opinion you are no better than tyrants."

Whether Cecile really intended to assassinate Robespierre remains unprovable; what is certain is that she did everything possible to incriminate herself as a royalist sympathizer and deliberately courted death. For political reasons, however, the Committee of Public Safety were determined to see her lone act as part of a foreign-financed plot to assassinate Republican leaders and reinstate the Bourbons. During the night of 24/25 May Cecile's father, brother and aunt were arrested without warning and warrants sent out for the detention of the two younger brothers. Despite intensive separate interrogations, however, no reliable evidence could be produced to prove that the entire family were implicated in Cecile's activities or that they had ever shown any but a passing interest in politics.

The family's utter bewilderment at Cecile's behaviour is vividly conveyed by the judicial records. She had assured her interrogators that she was a fervent royalist and devoutly religious; yet her father insisted (and in this he was independently supported by her brother) that:

He had never noticed any religious feelings in his daughter; that she had always seemed rather indifferent towards it; neither had she shown any signs of any other sort of fanaticism.

Antoine had always regarded his daughter as rather a frivolous girl and had indulged her little vanities. Testimonies from the Renaults' neighbours confirmed this. When one young woman visited the stationery shop to buy a pen, she was forced to listen for several minutes to Cecile's description of her latest fashionable hats and dresses. Neighbours also confirmed that she was rarely allowed out unchaperoned. The Renaults' lodger, Mademoiselle Papin, bore witness to the intense anxiety of Cecile's relations when it was discovered that she had gone out alone. Mlle Papin took it upon herself to search the neighbourhood. She made inquiries at the confectioner whose daughter was Cecile's

37 The Renault family were among the two thousand victims who perished on the Paris guillotine at the height of the Terror. Many were ordinary citizens who had fallen foul of members of the powerful Jacobin clique.

dressmaker, and at another seamstress whom Cecile sometimes employed. Final evidence for the innocence of the Renault relatives came again from Mlle Papin. Soon after she had gone to bed on the 24 May, she heard a knock at her door:

Who is there?
It is I, Mlle Papin (the voice of Jacques Renault)
Has Cecile come home?
No. I have brought you our cat. We have just been arrested.
Arrested! But why?
I do not know. Will you take care of our cat while we are away? Will you see that he has everything that he wants.

38 Fouquier-Tinville, dreaded prosecutor of the Revolutionary Tribunal

Only one useful piece of incriminating evidence came to light. In Antoine's desk lay a copy of a letter dated 4 January 1793, sent by him to his son, a corporal in the garrison at Berlimont:

I have seen your letter, in which you note that the citizens of the province in which you are would not wish the former king to be sentenced to death. At this present moment it is not possible to say anything to you on this matter, for nothing definite has yet been decided, but I think that, in the interests of the good and tranquillity of the Republic, it would not be desirable for him to be executed.

This reasonable assessment of the contemporary political situation was hardly the sentiment of a traitor, but in the atmosphere of 1794 it was sufficient to clinch the condemnation of a whole family.

On such slender evidence the four Renaults were tried, with fifty others previously unknown to them, before the Revolutionary Tribunal on 17 June. The charge was that they had made themselves:

enemies of the people by participating in the conspiracy of the foreigner; and attempting, by assassination, the fabrication and introduction of forged paper money and base coin, the depravement of morality and public spirit, and insurrection in the prisons – to promote civil war, dissolve the National Republic and re-establish royalty or any other tyrannical domination.

In accordance with a law passed only a week before, no defence was allowed; the accused were merely asked to plead "guilty" or "not guilty" to the charge. The prosecutor, Fouquier-Tinville, directed the jury to find all fifty-four guilty and duly pronounced sentence of death. Execution followed on the same day, the convicted being draped in the red cloaks of regicides. Witnesses have left admiring descriptions of the calm with which Cecile Renault faced death; of the last moments of her bewildered family, unwittingly caught up in her fate, no record remains. Only the two younger brothers escaped immediate execution, for they could not be brought to Paris in time for the trial and were saved by the downfall of Robespierre a month later.

Adrienne de Lafayette (1760-1807)

Married at fourteen, by 1789 Adrienne de Lafayette had spent fifteen years in the shadow of her famous husband, hero of the American War of Independence. Although intelligent and well-educated, she was little interested in politics; she devoted her life to home and children, and her faith in her husband's rightness remained absolute.

Longing for a peaceful private life, she regarded her husband's enthusiasm for the early stages of the revolution with a mixture of pride and trepidation. Her daughter, Virginie, later recalled:

She did the honours of her home in a way that charmed her numerous guests, but what she suffered in her heart was known only to those who heard her talk of her experiences. She saw my father at the head of a revolution, the end of which no-one could foretell. Every misfortune, every occasion of disorder, she watched with a clear and disillusioned eye. All through that time she was sustained by my father's principles, and was so wholly convinced of his power to do good

39 The Marquis de Lafayette.

and to prevent evil, that she suffered with unbelievable strength of character the constant dangers to which he was exposed. Not once in those days, she told us, did she see him leave the house without feeling that she might be saying goodbye to him for the last time. (Maurois, *Adrienne,* Cape, 1960)

When General de Lafayette tried to withdraw from politics in 1791, and settled in his country estate in central France, his wife was overjoyed; she wrote to her aunt:

We live here in a world of profound peace. M. de Lafayette revels in its delights as though he had never known a more active existence. His land, his house, Mademoiselle his aunt, his children and the writing of a few letters now fill his life completely. Only a war against the emigrés can tear him away, and I hope that nothing of that sort will happen.

By 1792, Lafayette – convinced that liberty with stability could only be achieved in France through a constitutional monarchy and fearing that a Republic would lead to extremism – had aroused the enmity of ardent revolutionaries and fled into exile. Virginie described Adrienne's anxiety during the days when she did not know whether or not her husband had reached safety:

Mama's face became paler and paler. At last she got up and we followed her to Mlle Marin's room. We had scarcely reached it when M. Frestel appeared with letters [telling of Lafayette's successful escape] . . . . Mama's joy was in proportion to the anxiety she had been feeling for the past few days.

That was not, however, the end of her problems. Proscribed as the wife of a traitor, Adrienne now found her own life under threat. Not only was Lafayette's property confiscated but also the dowry of his wife. In March 1793 she wrote to the friend who oversaw her financial affairs in Paris:

Not only is it brought home to me that I am completely ruined, but I realise that, after being compelled to treat with the Paris Commune, I shall still not see justice done.

Two months later this hitherto wealthy woman tried urgently to raise one hundred louis to settle her debts and pay the wages of her servants; then she threw herself on the charity of her parents.

Convinced of her own innocence, she little realized the personal danger involved in being related to a "traitor". In April 1793 she wrote to her friend:

Honestly, my dear friend, you must be mad to be so concerned about the trouble in Lozère. I beg you to be persuaded once and for all that the peace of our canton is unbroken . . . . Moreover, since all my neighbours know perfectly well that my patriotism is genuine, I am safe from all suspicion.

Under the Law of Suspects she was arrested in September 1793. Even as she was about to be transferred to Paris from the local prison in May 1794 she maintained a naive belief that legal processes and natural justice still counted for something. She sent a petition to local Republicans:

It is a matter of no little distress to me that my conduct should be investigated in the one place [Paris] of all others where it is least known. I would have counted it a great gain to have gathered around me those who have been in a position to observe, since those days when I believed that I might be of service to the Republic, whether the violence of my personal sufferings had changed for the worse those feelings of mine which were well-known to all with whom I came into contact.

But separated though I am from those places in which I have lived since misfortune came upon me, it is my duty to hope that truth will triumph. I beg you therefore to collect honest testimonies in my favour, so that even though it is no longer possible for you to decide my fate, you may at least be able to enlighten those into whose hands I am to be committed of the facts. It is my children who ask justice of you.

Adrienne's hope of justice had little justification. She spent over a year in the Plessis Prison in Paris, in daily expectation of execution. Her grandmother, mother and sister all perished at the guillotine, on a single day in May 1794. Her daughters were forced to live on local charity. Virginie wrote:

We live off the money which the village people have lent with such touching eagerness to my aunt. Every day we are told that she and my sister are to be sent to the house of detention at Brioude, and that my brother and I are to be confined in the poorhouse.

40 At the height of the Terror, few of the aristocrats who had remained in France escaped imprisonment and death.

The tragedy that had swept her family triggered off a deep depression in the normally serene Adrienne. The American ambassador, Monroe, who visited her in prison, was shocked by the change in her. Following her release in May 1795, the struggle for survival continued. Virginie wrote to her great-aunt:

We are going tomorrow to the former château. We have a bedroom with Mama, a closet, a cabinet and a room for when my uncle de Grammont comes. Besides the furniture and the mattresses which we have got back, we have bought many kitchen things and six chairs.

When Adrienne made a journey to Paris to obtain a passport, she was forced to make the trip on foot.

In September 1795, this dutiful wife, accompanied by her daughters, left France to join her husband, then imprisoned by the Austrian authorities at Olmutz. Conditions there were as bad as those in Paris gaols and completed the damage done to Adrienne's health. She developed scurvy, and by the end of 1796 her health had deteriorated to such an extent that she was forced to dictate the following letter to her daughter:

It is now nearly two months since your kind letter reached me. I am, however, deprived of the pleasure of answering it myself. Because of the worsening condition of my blood and of the excessively insanitary condition of this prison, my arms have been for some time unbelievably swollen and my fingers incapable of movement .... My skin is peeling .... The pain, the impossibility of closing my hands and the spasms in my whole nervous system make my life more than a little disagreeable.

The Lafayette family were finally released in 1797, eventually to return to France and a long struggle to retrieve the family fortunes. Adrienne never fully recovered from the damage done to her health by the prison systems of two countries and died prematurely in 1807, thirty years before her husband.

Grace Dalrymple Elliot (1758-1823)

It could be argued that Grace Elliot brought upon herself many of the tribulations that she suffered between 1789 and 1795. Although she had long been resident in France and was an intimate friend of the Duke of Orleans, she was also a British citizen and escape from France before 1793 would have been a relatively simple matter. However, not only did she choose to remain, but she was outspoken in her opposition to the revolution and reckless in the assistance she gave to those whose lives were threatened by it. Her adventures, as revealed in her memoirs, give a fascinating picture of the wide variety of people who fell victim to the years of terror.

As early as the storming of the Tuileries in August 1792, Grace Elliot showed an unerring instinct for getting involved in risky situations. The major commanding the palace guard lived near her and:

In the course of the morning I had an opportunity of being of use to three or four Swiss soldiers, whom I hid in my house until the evening; Major Beckman living in the Rue Verte, and his garden and mine joining, they had come over the wall. I wish I could have done as much for their major, but he, poor man, perished the same day. I don't know whether the men who were hidden in my house escaped. They would go away in the evening and I never heard of them more.

Her reputation as an intrepid royalist must have spread, for shortly afterwards Chansenets, former governor of the Tuileries, came to her in secret and begged her to help him escape from Paris. While he was in her house, Grace was warned that a street-by-street search by the local Revolutionary Guard was in progress, and she was forced to hide Chansenets under the mattress on her bed, while she herself:

passed a most miserable night, surrounded by my servants, and almost in fits myself at the idea

41 The taking of the Tuileries in 1792. Only a few of its defenders were lucky enough to escape the fury of the mob.

of the horrid visit I was going to receive. I trembled so much that I could hardly keep in bed, and the unfortunate man who was the cause of my misery I thought perhaps had died near me, for I could not hear him breathe at times.

Fortunately, the guards:

only felt the top of my bed and at its feet, then under the bed. They also undid all the sofa cushions, both in my room and in my drawing room, looking into my bathroom and, in short, were an hour and a half in my room.

Grace was so angry at the indignities she suffered that she was tempted to give herself up in defiance; she resisted the temptation because:

Although my own life was of little value, still I had no reason to suppose that the unfortunate man near me did not value his.

Her assessment was correct, for Chansenets did not share Grace's coolness and contempt for safety. When the search ended, she and her maid found him:

in a high fever and almost delirious and crying; in short he was in a most dreadful state. We were distracted for fear of a discovery; had he died, where could we have put him, or what could we have done?

Chansenets was eventually smuggled to safety in England, but the shadow of suspicion remained on Grace and she was subject to regular nightly visits by the Revolutionary Guard, who ransacked her house for incriminating papers and hoarded food. The inevitable arrest came in the summer of 1793, and Grace Elliot spent thirty uncomfortable hours in a local prison, awaiting examination. The conditions she described were experienced by many victims of the Terror. In one room:

there were at least two hundred – a great many women and many of them of high rank. During

42 Terrifying house-searches were a common feature of the Terror.

the whole time I was there, which was thirty hours, I was close to the poor Duchesse de Grammont and the Duchesse de Chatelet. I believe that there were not ten chairs in the room and the women were fainting from fatigue. The Duchesse de Grammont was terribly bulky and her legs were terribly swollen.

From nine o'clock in the morning of Friday to twelve o'clock on Saturday morning did I remain on my legs, except for about five minutes now and then when these ladies pulled me on to their knees, but I was so much afraid of hurting them that it was no ease to me.

Released shortly afterwards, Grace was re-arrested in September 1793, transferred to Carmes Prison in Paris and remained there for eighteen months. On one occasion she shared a cell with General Hoche, who had been promoted from the ranks to command the Army of the Rhine and had once been fêted as a hero of the Republic. A quarrel with the powerful Saint-Just had led to his disgrace and arrest. Grace told him:

General, if you know me, you cannot be surprised to see me here; but I assure you that I am much surprised to see you, for I thought you one of the defenders of the revolution. "So I am", said he, "but they seem to forget and oppress their real friends; however, I hope that I shall not be here long; I have been cruelly slandered."

Hoche was released and reinstated four months later, when Saint-Just fell from power, but others were not so fortunate. Another temporary cell-mate of Grace Elliot was Josephine de Beauharnais – the future Empress – and her husband, Alexandre. The arbitrariness that governed their fate is shown by the following incident:

The Convention imagined, or pretended to imagine, that there was a conspiracy in our prison. We were all denounced by Barère; and they asserted that we had laid a plan to set fire to the prison. In short, so cruel yet absurd was the accusation that when the Comité du Salut Public [Committee of Public Safety] sent for fifty prisoners out of our room to be tried for the conspiracy, the gaoler, who was a horrid Jacobin, laughed at the soldiers and said, "A conspiracy! Why the prisoners here are all as quiet as lambs". However, fifty were led out of our prison to the scaffold for that same conspiracy.

Among those executed were Alexandre de Beauharnais and:

a young Englishman of the name of Harrop, who had been sent to the Irish College for his education, and whose parents had never sent for him home. He had been imprudent and had abused the Republic in some coffee house, in consequence of which he was arrested. He was only eighteen years old.

One particularly grisly incident occurred:

43 During her eighteen months in prison Grace Elliot saw many of her companions depart in the tumbril on their way to the guillotine. Only luck saved her from a similar fate.

Two other young men, in going down the prison stairs, which were formed like a well, took hold of each other's hands and leaped down. They were dashed to pieces; but as the number was to be fifty, they took two other people to make up the number.

The prisoners lived in fear not only of official execution, but also of a repeat of the September massacres. Grace herself was scheduled for the guillotine on 27 July and had had her hair shorn in preparation. On that day, however, Robespierre fell from power, her execution was deferred, and she was eventually released in the spring of 1795. This time she fled to the safety of England, where she wrote her memoirs at the request of George III. A Francophile to the end, however, she returned to France after the Bourbon restoration and lived there until her death in 1823.

THE SURVIVORS

Although the rapid political changes of the revolutionary period created many casualties, there were those who managed to survive and prosper under successive governments of very different political complexions. Some survivors were clever time-servers, interested only in furthering their careers; others appear to have been sincere in their devotion to the revolution, and it is often difficult to judge whether luck or an unprincipled desire for self-preservation was the more responsible for their ability to adapt to the post-revolutionary situation. After the coup of Thermidor, many of those most closely associated with the Terror followed Robespierre to the guillotine; among them were Fouquier-Tinville, the Public Prosecutor, and Carrier, the notorious Representative at Nantes. However, Fouché, closely implicated in similar massacres at Lyons, survived and prospered, as did the artist David.

The army provided somewhat different examples. The revolutionary system of rapid promotion from the ranks opened up undreamt-of career opportunities for talented but untitled soldiers. After a decade of frustration in the royal army, future Marshals Massena and Bernadotte both experienced

45 On his way to the top: Napoleon Bonaparte as Commander in Chief of the Army of Italy, 1797.

44 Fouquier-Tinville on trial for his life after Thermidor.

meteoric rises in the Republican Army. With France involved almost continuously in foreign wars from 1792 onwards, it was easier for soldiers than for politicians to ride out political storms, as indispensible patriots serving France rather than faction. Carnot, of the Committee of Public Safety, used his reputation as a military genius to survive the fall of Robespierre, become one of the five heads of state under the Directory, and serve, for a short while, as Napoleon's War Minister. Moreover, while later generations have condemned his contemporaries as the authors of the Terror, Carnot has preserved his reputation as a sincere and dedicated Republican, who, nevertheless, concentrated on apolitical military matters and kept aloof from bloodthirsty Parisian politics.

The best example of a career carved out of the revolution is, of course, that of Napoleon Bonaparte. Only twenty in 1789, he had risen to the rank of General of Brigade by 1794. The disgrace of Augustin Robespierre – brother of the dictator, Representative on Mission to the Army in the South, and Napoleon's patron – brought Napoleon close to the guillotine himself in 1794; his saviour was Barras, Thermidorian conspirator and new commander of the Army of the Interior, who was an admirer of Napoleon's military talents. Within the year Napoleon had become Barras' second-in-command in Paris. The abortive royalist rising of Vendémiaire was Napoleon's first great opportunity to make a decisive impact on politics. When the defeat of the coup broke the power of Paris to decide the course of French politics and paved the way for a new constitution – the Directory – Napoleon was rewarded by promotion to the rank of Major-General and succeeded Barras (who became one of the five Directors) in command of the Army of the Interior. In 1796 political influence helped him to gain command of the French armies in Italy. Spectacular victories in Italy, which enabled France to impose the humiliating Treaty of Campo Formio on Austria, won Napoleon the loyalty of the Army and made him a popular hero. By contrast, the prestige of the Directory fell ever lower between 1795 and 1799; Jacobinism revived in Paris; royalist uprisings occurred in Brittany and the South-West; and public desire for strong and stable government escalated. Napoleon was in a strong position to make a bid for power. In the coup of Brumaire, he established himself as virtual dictator, with the title of First Consul, and with this the true revolution can be said to have ended. However, it was not until the collapse of his Empire in 1815 that the Bourbons were fully restored, so completing the cycle of events that had begun in 1789.

Joseph Fouché (1759-1820)

Fouché's survival was remarkable. From his early career as the principal of a religious school, to his peaceful death in Italy in 1820, he had trodden the path of revolutionary fanatic and executioner, desperate fugitive and minister of police. At different times, he numbered among his enemies, Robespierre:

Within the space of a fortnight Fouché's head must fall on the scaffold, or mine will.

Napoleon:

I should have hanged him; that was my intention. If I had won at Waterloo I would have had him shot.

and Chateaubriand:

A hyena in human clothes, thief, atheist, assassin.

Even his first biographer, Martel, wrote that he was:

one of the most villainous, most infamous of all the monsters in human guise of that redoubtable period.

Perhaps it was the revolution itself that made Fouché such an expert survivor. He had a stroke of luck in his early career when, as a teacher, he met Robespierre, his sister Charlotte and Lazare Carnot. An affection grew between him and Charlotte, who saw in him "the most ardent patriotism, the most

46 Fouché only narrowly escaped the fate of Fouquier-Tinville, but survived to become one of the most renowned and feared men of the Napoleonic Empire.

sacred devotion". This did not last. Later Charlotte wrote: "He so cleverly concealed his vile sentiments and evil passions from my eyes, as from the eyes of my brother, that I was his dupe, as was Maximilien." In September 1792 he was elected as one of the eight deputies representing Nantes, and voted for the execution of Louis in 1793. He later justified his action by saying:

I meant to strike less at the monarch than at the Crown.

Later in 1793 he was chosen by the Convention as a Commissioner to Brittany and the Vendée, to instruct "the fellow citizens on the new dangers that threaten the country". Arriving at Nantes, he took control in order to defend the town against the royalists, calling on the people to:

Take action, march to victory – or wait by your fireside for all the anguish of ignominy and death . . . keep the strictest watch on the rich, the monopolists, the priests . . . . Denounce them on the spot to the nation's justice. Close your ranks,

and if you find among you those who are timid or cowardly, run them through with the republican weapon, the bayonet.

Years later he said of such language:

These commonplace expressions . . . which in calmer times arouse a sort of horror . . . were, so to speak, official phrases.

His most infamous actions were those performed at Lyons, where he had been dispatched by the Committee of Public Safety with Collot d'Herbois, armed with the power to destroy the city, because "Lyons made war on liberty". The two men developed a system of mass execution:

To make execution swift and more impressive in the eyes of the people . . . chain them together and arrange them in lines along which cannon loaded with grapeshot will fire.

Collot boasted: "We blasted 200 at a time",

47 Fouché shared responsibility with Collot d'Herbois for the massacres at Lyons in 1793 and they were fellow conspirators in the plot of Thermidor. Yet, while Fouché's career flourished, Collot died in exile in Guiana.

although Fouché in his memoirs argued that it had not been *his* idea and claimed:

I never held during the reign of terror the helm of power; on the contrary, I was myself a sufferer by it.

As it was in Fouché's best interests thereafter to disown this part of his career, this justification cannot be accepted at face value, but it seems likely that Fouché tried to impress his superiors in Paris by appearing more bloodthirsty than he actually was; the 213 executions that he claimed in his reports have since been found to be only 64.

In June 1794 Robespierre recalled Fouché. The reasons for this remain unclear. Possibly the exaggerated accounts of his zeal at Lyons had convinced Robespierre that Fouché and Collot, like Carrier at Nantes, were getting out of control and alienating loyal Lyonnaises as well as eliminating disloyal ones. Perhaps Charlotte's antagonism towards her erstwhile friend helped to poison her brother's mind. For two months, Fouché feared for his life; he moved from house to house, fearing even to sleep a night at home, while Robespierre's agents searched for him. While he fled, he became one of the instigators of a conspiracy to overthrow the dictator. By the beginning of July both men realized that they were fighting for their existence. While Robespierre issued a warrant naming Fouché as "the leader of a conspiracy we have to overthrow", his opponents outwitted him. Fouché was not yet safe, however; the coup of Thermidor produced a backlash against *all* who had been associated with the Terror.

Fouché was never arrested, perhaps because he had too much information at his disposal and would be prepared to take many other people along with him to the guillotine. He demonstrated his continuing potential by informing on an attempted royalist coup, which was put down in October 1795 by Napoleon Bonaparte. He worked hard to gain the friendship of Barras, soon to become a Directorate member, and was rewarded by being given the temporary post of government agent to the 10th and 11th Divisions at Narbonne. However, this was clearly seen as an humiliation by Fouché, who wrote in his memoirs:

Under a government of which I was one of the founders, I was, if not proscribed, at least in complete disgrace.

Worse was to come, as, when his job ended in 1796, he was simply ignored; presumably, it was thought that he would be no great threat to anyone else if his life was not in danger. Fouché had made so little out of the revolution that he now had to try to make his living by breeding pigs and spinning flax. He begged his only potential supporter, Barras, to give him another chance. As Barras said, Fouché was:

in the direst distress . . . perpetually pestering me to give him any kind of place.

It would be interesting to speculate whether Napoleon gave any support, as he had clearly gained from Fouché's betrayal of the Royalists in October 1795. Certainly it is difficult otherwise to explain how it was that Fouché's fortunes so rapidly improved. Barras relented, and gave him a post as one of the civil contractors to the army (traditionally a means of making money quickly) and also asked that he worked undercover for the Ministry of Police. This was a great opportunity to regain influence, and also to gain the wealth that Fouché now saw to be essential for survival. A combination of political and financial skill was rewarded by his being granted the ambassadorship (effectively governorship) of the Cisalpine Republic and then of Holland. Then came his greatest coup – the gaining of the post of Minister of Police. Barras thought him the most capable man for the post, and Foreign Minister, Talleyrand, said:

At a time when the Jacobins are showing themselves so audacious, none but a Jacobin can knock them down. There is no better man than Fouché.

From 1799 to 1802 he was the most feared

secret policeman in Europe, whilst living a life of the utmost domestic tranquillity with his wife, children and a few old friends. He served as a senator between 1802 and 1804, and was then reappointed as Minister of Police. Created Duke of Otranto in 1806, he was governor of Rome from 1810 to 1815, and with the support of the Comte d'Artois remained in that post under Louis XVIII. He knew so much about so many people that none dared attack him; Fouché had become the archetypal secret policeman whom none could do without.

André Massena (1758-1817) and Jean-Baptiste Bernadotte (1763-1844)

André Massena's parents were small shopkeepers in the town of Nice, then in the Kingdom of Sardinia. Bored at the prospect of a tradesman's life, Massena ran away to sea at the age of thirteen. Four years later he joined the Royal Italian Regiment, a sort of foreign legion, recruited from Italians and Sardinians for service under the kings of France. He taught himself to read and write, rose to the rank of sergeant and earned a reputation as a competent instructor in military tactics. His commanding officer recognized his value to the army; once, after an incompetently-executed series of manoeuvres, he berated his junior officers:

Your ignorance about tactics is disgraceful, gentlemen; any of your subordinates, Massena for example, could manoeuvre the batallion better than you have done.

The system of aristocratic privilege, however, made further promotion impossible, and Massena resigned in indignation in 1789 and opened a grocer's shop in Antibes in southern France. When the National Assembly called for 100,000 volunteers in January 1791 to defend the frontiers and replace unreliable units of the regular army, Massena's chance had come. As a man of military experience, he was given the immediate rank of lieutenant, and a year later, following the practice of the early Republican Army, he was elevated by his fellow soldiers to the command of the batallion, with the rank of lieutenant-colonel. A report of the proceedings was sent to Paris:

The vote was taken in the manner prescribed. The President asked if anyone had anything to say before closing the box; on receiving no answer, he ordered the count. Of 465 votes, Citizen Massena had 431. Citizen Massena had an absolute majority.

For the next six years, Massena fought the Austrians in northern Italy, helping, along the way, to annex his native Nice to France. His reputation as a. brilliant field commander spread to Paris. At the capture of Toulon, the Representatives on Mission to the Army, sent the following dispatch:

In the name of the French people; from the people's representatives attached to the army at Toulon.
 As a result of the report rendered to them by the general commanding the Army of Italy present at Toulon, of the courage, zeal and skill shown by Citizen Massena in the struggle against this rebel city, the undersigned

nominate Citizen Massena for promotion to the rank of General of Division.

The future course of Massena's career did not run altogether smoothly. In 1796 he expected to be given command of the Army of Italy, only to be passed over in favour of Napoleon, eleven years his junior. As the latter rose to be dictator of France, the relationship between the two men remained uneasy, yet Napoleon was forced to acknowledge, grudgingly, Massena's gifts as a commander:

He had a strong constitution and would ride recklessly night and day over rocks and through the mountains; that was the kind of war that he specialised in and understood thoroughly ... his outstanding quality was doggedness; he was never discouraged. He was slack about discipline and negligent in administration ... but at the first sound of a gun, in the midst of cannon balls and danger, his thoughts acquired strength and clarity. If he were defeated, he would return to the charge as though he were the victor.

In 1799 Massena finally became Commander in Italy and, eventually, Marshal of France. By 1809 he had also acquired the title of Prince of Esserling and had become one of the wealthiest men in Europe – only to see rank and wealth disappear with the Bourbon restoration. Wellington, who fought against Massena in the Peninsula campaign, paid a high tribute to the former cabin boy made good:

I would say, as far as my own experience goes, that he was one of their very best.

Jean-Baptiste Bernadotte

The career of Jean-Baptiste Bernadotte followed a similar but even more illustrious route. In spite of commendations from three successive colonels of regiment, there was no chance that Sergeant Bernadotte's fourteen years of service (1775-89) in the royalist army would be rewarded with a commission. Frustration converted him into an ardent

48 Marshal Massena.

49 Marshal Bernadotte, future King of Sweden.

Republican. When he finally became an officer, under the conditions of 1792, he wrote to his brother:

I hope soon to be captain. I am at present 4th Lieutenant. But these reflections do not please me so much as the thought of Liberty, of which I know today the precious worth.

Bernadotte's military career ended on a high note when Napoleon gave him the throne of Sweden. Showing considerable political skill, he survived Napoleon's defeat, and his descendants rule Sweden today.

Cochon de Lapperant

Up to 1789, Cochon was a respectable provincial lawyer in moderately comfortable circumstances, seemingly condemned to a dull and predictable career. Election to the Estates General gave him an unexpected opportunity to pursue political ambitions and indulge a hitherto unrevealed lust for power. As a deputy to the Convention, he voted for the King's death, and, having established himself in the favour of the Jacobins, was sent as Representative on Mission to Valenciennes, at a time when panic threatened to engulf the town at the news of the approaching Austrian army. Cochon proved himself to be a competent and forceful administrator and he was determined that future changes of government should not wreck his promising career. Surviving the fall of Robespierre, he advanced to become Prefect of Antwerp under the Empire.

The Bourbon restoration drove all regicides, including Cochon, into exile. Due to influential connections, however, he was one of the few able to return to France, and he lived until his death in reasonable security and comfort. Cobb describes him as one of those people who are "capable of adjusting themselves to the passage of time" and says that, with Cochon, it was "a matter of turning terror on or off, as from a tap, according to the circumstances". He could be relied upon "to defend, if necessary ruthlessly, established authority". (*Reactions to the French Revolution*, O.U.P., 1972)

Biographical Notes On Other Personalities Of The Revolution

Artois, Comte de (1757-1836) The future Charles X of France (1824-30), Charles was brother to Louis XVI and Louis XVIII, whom he succeeded in 1824. Before the revolution his reputation had been that of a reactionary and dissolute prince. He fled France in 1789 and proved a great embarrassment to his elder brother because of his overtly anti-revolutionary views. He travelled in the Austrian Netherlands, Italy, Prussia and Russia before settling in Edinburgh, where he remained until 1814. He never went back on his extreme royalist position and was always an enemy of reform. He in turn was overthrown by revolution, but escaped to recommence his exile in Edinburgh.

50 Artois and the other emigrés painted the revolution in the most bloodthirsty light and did much to influence public opinion in England against developments in France. Here is an English cartoonist's impression of the common people of Paris.

Barère de Vieuzac, Bertrand (1755-1841) Barère was active in politics long before the revolution and served as a member of the Parlement of Toulouse before being elected to the Estates General in 1789. He founded a journal, *Le Point du Jour*, and joined the Jacobin Club. At about the same time, he was appointed tutor to Pamela, natural daughter of the duc d'Orleans. He became a tribunal judge in 1791 and a Convention Deputy in 1792. Barère voted for the execution of Louis XVI in 1793 and took a leading role in the campaign against the Girondins. As a member of the Committee of Public Safety, he earned the approval of Robespierre, producing over 200 reports. At the Thermidor coup of 1794 he deserted Robespierre, but this did not save him from imprisonment. He later escaped and spent five years in hiding in Bordeaux, scraping a living by writing and gradually selling his possessions. His fortunes improved during the Empire, when he was employed as a secret agent. However, the Restoration saw him exiled as a regicide. He was allowed to return in 1830 and was given a small allowance by Louis Philippe before his death in 1841.

Barras, Paul François Jean, Vicomte de (1755-1829) An aristocrat who had served in India and fought at the battle of Pondicherry. Disillusioned, he had turned to politics, and the revolution saw him as a member of the Convention and sitting with the Jacobins. He became a Representative of the Convention in the disciplining of Marseilles (c.f. the actions of Fouché and Collot d'Herbois in Lyons), working with the Jacobin journalist Louis Fréron, who was a friend of Robespierre. When Toulon was captured from the British by Bonaparte in 1793, Barras was set to pacify that city as well. He played a leading role in suppressing the 1795 Vendémiaire revolt, being given command of the troops loyal to the Convention. Bonaparte was his second-in-command. From 1795 to 1799 Barras was one of the five-man Directorate, and worked with Sièyes assisting Bonaparte in the coup 18th Brumaire.

51 Barras in the robes of a member of the Directorate.

Brissot de Warville, Jacques Pierre (1754-93) Perhaps the leading member of the so-called Girondin Party, Brissot is best known for his advocacy of war as a means of national regeneration – and this led him into conflict with Robespierre. He said: "A people which, after a thousand years of slavery, has achieved liberty, needs war. It needs war to consolidate its freedom." Brissot was a typical revolutionary in his origins. His father had run a cookshop in Chartres, and had sent his son to Law School. He turned to journalism and pamphleteering, and travelled in England (where he was imprisoned for debt), the USA and Switzerland. Returning to France, he became a confidant of the duc d'Orleans and was imprisoned in the Bastille for sedition. His newspaper, *Patriote Français*, became the leading Girondist publication. His enthusiasm for a war of regeneration backfired on him when the 1793 Dumouriez offensive collapsed. Unrepentant of his policy, he called for war with England. Accused by the Jacobins of betraying the revolution he was executed in 1793.

Carnot, Lazare Nicolas Marguerite (1753-1823) Carnot was an Engineer Officer in the Royal Army, with an international reputation as a soldier-scholar – so much so that he was offered a post in Prussia by that country's ruler, Frederick the Great. Carnot turned it down, because he could not bear the idea of serving any country but his own. This patriotism did not extend to loyalty to his King, and as a member of the Convention he voted for Louis' execution. He made his name as a military planner, and, in particular, masterminded the Flanders campaign. However, Thermidor saw him struggling for his life and it took an impassioned plea from one Deputy – "Carnot has organized victory" – to stave off a vote for his prescription. His fortunes ebbed and flowed until the Consulate, when he was favoured by Napoleon and so became War Minister in 1800 and Minister of the Interior during the 100 Days. He briefly headed the government of France after Napoleon's final abdication, only to be exiled by Louis XVIII. Carnot died in Prussia in 1823.

Chartres, Louis Philippe, Duke of (1773-1850) Eldest son of Philippe Egalité, he shared his father's identification with the Jacobin cause, joining the Jacobin Club in 1791 and fighting the Army of the Republic at Valmy and Jemappes. When his father was arrested in April 1793, however, Chartres protected his own life by fleeing into Austrian territory (his two younger brothers were both imprisoned) and only returned to France in 1815. Thereafter, he continued the family tradition of opposing the reigning Bourbon monarch, by supporting the demand of the middle classes for greater political representation. His chance came with the deposition of Charles X in 1830, when middle-class acclaim made Louis Philippe the first and last Orleanist king of France. However, he too was forced to abdicate after the revolution of 1848 and died in exile in England.

Collot d'Herbois, Jean-Marie (1749-96) An actor and dramatist who used his oratorical powers to become a favourite of the Paris mob. As a member of the radical Paris Commune of 1792, he helped organize the August invasion of the Tuileries and supported the September Massacres. His election to the Committee of Public Safety in July 1793 was probably intended both to distract his attention from Parisian mob politics and to channel him into activities approved by the government. Dispatched as Representative on Mission with Fouché to Lyons in November 1793, he organized the bloody purge of dissidents that culminated in the mass shootings of 4-5 December 1793. Collot's excessive violence and his enthusiasm for dechristianization prompted the Committee to recall him in March 1794. Collot had always resented Robespierre's pre-eminence and this antagonism was now sharpened; when his friends, the Hébertists, were eliminated, Collot joined the conspiracy that was to culminate in the overthrow of Robespierre and his supporters in July 1794. In the post-Thermidorian, anti-Jacobin backlash, however, Collot himself was indicted and deported to Guiana, where he died of yellow fever.

Couthon, Georges (1755-94) Georges Couthon was a lawyer and an advocate for the poor at Clermont-Ferrand from 1788-90. He was appointed President of the Clermont-Ferrand Tribunal in 1790. As an Assembly Deputy in 1791, he spoke out against Lafayette and in favour of "patriot" soldiers who had mutinied. Elected to the Convention, he was vigorous in demanding the execution of Louis and a bitter opponent of the Girondins. His motion of June 1793 initiated the purge against them. A member of the Committee of Public Safety, he was entrusted with directing the recapture of Lyons, though he had no stomach for the ferocious revenge which the Committee wished to visit upon that city after its capture. Replaced by Collot and Fouché, he returned to Paris and helped Robespierre and Saint-Just in the extermination of Danton and the Hébertists. He was responsible for the 1794 Law of Prairial which speeded up the work of the Revolutionary Tribunal. Although not as violent in practice as in speech, his pursuit of those he considered enemies of the revolution ensured his downfall with Robespierre and Saint-Just. He was guillotined in July 1794.

Danton, Georges (1759-94) A prominent member of the National Convention, a forceful orator and colourful personality, Danton was the first of the popular Jacobin leaders. He was a founder-member of the Committee of

52 Danton, one of the revolution's most powerful orators.

Public Safety, but by mid-1793 he had broken with Robespierre in a quarrel caused partly by a clash of personalities and partly by political differences. Although no pacifist (it was rumoured that he had refused to allow the Paris municipal authorities to control the September Massacres, saying "I don't care a damn for the prisoners; let them shift for themselves"), Danton finally recoiled from the intensification of the Terror, made his distaste public, and found himself and his closest friends arraigned under the Law of Suspects before the Revolutionary Tribunal in March 1794. He was guillotined on 6 April 1794.

Desmoulins, Camille (1760-94) An unemployed lawyer, who first attracted public attention on 12 July 1789, when he leapt on to a chair in the gardens of the Palais Royale, plucked a horsechestnut leaf to wear in his hat as a cockade, and invited the crowd to resist a rumoured counter-attack by royalist forces against the newly-created Assembly. This was the beginning of the popular uprising that led to the fall of the Bastille, the withdrawal of royal troops from Paris, and the domination of the Paris mob over the course of the revolution. Thereafter, Desmoulins kept in the forefront of revolutionary politics through the production of *Le Vieux Cordelier*, a newspaper identifying primarily with the Dantonist point of view. In the spring of 1794 he supported Danton's call for a lessening of the Terror and was executed with him in April 1794.

Fouquier-Tinville, Antoine-Quentin (1746-95) After a relatively unsuccessful ten years in minor legal posts Fouquier-Tinville was appointed Public Prosecutor to the Revolutionary Tribunal in May 1793; his function was to select the suspects to be brought to trial and to prepare the case against them, a task which he performed with enthusiasm and energy, becoming one of the most feared men in France. He boasted that between May 1793 and July 1794 he condemned more than 2,400 suspects to death, including Marie Antoinette and Danton. Himself brought to trial after the coup of Thermidor, he argued that he had only been acting on the orders of the Committees of Public Safety and General Security, but this defence was not accepted and he was executed in 1795.

Hérault de Séchelles, Marie-Jean (1759-94) Hérault was a turncoat who failed to make the right move at a critical moment and thus shared the fate of the royal family whom he betrayed. A courtier, Hérault was related to the Polignac family and a favourite of Marie Antoinette. King's Attorney in 1777, he became Attorney General to the Paris parlement in 1785. In 1789 he broke with the court, and took part in the attack on the Bastille. 1791 saw him Deputy for Paris, and eventually Chairman of the Jacobin Club. A member of the Convention, he was dispatched to the new department of Mont-Blanc and was still with the Army of the Alps when the King was tried and executed. Hérault was President of the Convention during the overthrow of the Girondins, and by July 1793 a member of the Committee of Public Safety. Apparently well-entrenched in the revolutionary hierarchy, in fact he had many enemies. His life-style, involving secret relations with emigrés and a number of love affairs, made him unpopular with more conventional, and less well-born, revolutionaries. He fell with Danton in April 1794.

Hoche, Louis-Lazare (1768-97) The son of a royal stableman, Hoche had enlisted as a trooper in the French Guard in 1784. The abolition of the aristocratic monopoly over commissions and his own distinguished service against the Austrians (1792-93) led to Hoche's appointment in 1793 as general commanding the Army of the Moselle. In 1794, however, he quarrelled with his colleague, General Pichegru, who denounced him to Saint-Just as a traitor and had him imprisoned. Hoche survived to resume his military career after the coup of Thermidor and was appointed commander of the Army of the Rhine in 1797. As a popular general, with many troops under his command, he gave valuable assistance to Bonaparte in purging the Convention of its royalist elements during the coup of Fruchtidor, and many believed that the two generals were destined to become rivals in the struggle for political supremacy in France. This danger was removed, however, when Hoche died of pneumonia in September 1797.

Josephine, Empress (1763-1814) Born Marie Josephine Tascher de la Pagerie, in the French colony of Martinique, she married in 1779 Vicomte Alexandre de Beauharnais. Although the latter served loyally and with distinction in the armies of the Republic, both husband and wife were arrested as aristocrats in late 1793. Alexandre de Beauharnais was executed, but Josephine herself survived to be released after Thermidor. Mistress of the influential Barras and a leader of fashionable Parisian society under the Directory, she married General Bonaparte, four years her junior, in 1796 and was crowned Empress of the French in 1804. The childless marriage was annulled in 1810, in order to allow Bonaparte to contract a more advantageous alliance with Marie Louise, daughter of the Emperor of Austria.

Lafayette, Marie Joseph Paul Yves Roch Gilbert du Motier, Marquis de (1757-1834) A French nobleman who distinguished himself in the army of the American colonists in the War of Independence (1776-83) and brought back to France the idea of liberty and the rights of citizens against autocratic governments. In 1789 he became the first commander of the National Guard, but in 1791 he lost popular support when he ordered troops to fire on anti-royalist demonstrators in the Champs de Mars (*see* Glossary – National Guard). Fearing for his safety, and himself disillusioned with the direction the revolution was taking, he fled to Austrian protection in 1792, only to be imprisoned at Olmutz as a dangerous radical. Released in 1797, he lived in retirement under Napoleon, but returned to political life after 1815 and played a prominent part in the deposition of Charles X and the installation of Louis Philippe.

Marat, Jean Paul (1743-93) A doctor by profession, Marat became a leader of the sans-culottes movement, and his newspaper *L'ami du Peuple* ("The People's Friend") was, for a while, the most influential of the radical Parisian journals. Regarded by many as the chief instigator of the September Massacres and the most bloodthirsty of the revolutionaries, he was assassinated in July 1793 by a disillusioned Girondin, Charlotte Corday, and became, in revolutionary circles, a popular martyr.

Marie Antoinette, Queen of France (1755-93) Marie Antoinette, daughter of Francis I and Maria Theresa of Austria, was deeply unpopular in pre-revolutionary France, though Jefferson's claim that, without her, there would have been no revolution is an overstatement. She had married the Dauphin (the future Louis XVI) at the age of fifteen and was expected to behave like a mature woman when her interests and enthusiasms where those of a healthy adolescent. As she grew up in the court, she gradually became a political queen, though not necessarily a wise one. However, Louis gave no direction, and she dominated him easily. Her brother-in-law, Charles d'Artois, became a close friend, and she did her best to control the appointment of the King's ministers. She was largely responsible for the unfortunate replacement of Turgot by Calonne as finance minister. The combination of such political activity with her reputation for extravagance and immorality made her a prime target in the early days of the revolution, and it was largely against her that the women of Paris marched when they invaded the palace of Versailles in 1789. She masterminded the abortive flight to Varennes in 1791, and was eventually guillotined in 1793. Her body was exhumed and honourably re-interred during the Restoration.

Napoleon Bonaparte, Napoleon I, Emperor of the French (1769-1821) Napoleon's seizure of power by the Brumaire coup of 1799 can be seen as the formal end of the revolutionary Republic that had begun ten years before. However, it was not until 1804 that he crowned himself Emperor, in the presence of Pope Pius VII.

Like Carnot, Napoleon had begun his career in a technical branch of the Royal Army (in this case, the artillery) rather than in a more prestigious infantry or cavalry unit. He served the Republic from the beginning and his role in the recapture of Toulon from the British in 1793 won him promotion to brigadier general. He narrowly missed disgrace, or worse, in the Thermidor coup, but regained confidence as Barras' second-in-command in Paris, and his reputation was made in the Italian campaign of 1796. His Egyptian campaign turned out to be a disaster, after a promising start, but he was able to overthrow the Directory in 1799 in the Brumaire coup d'état and establish the Consulate (serving with Sièyes and Ducos). In December 1799 he became 1st Consul (Consul for life in 1802). During the Consulate came his greatest achievements – the Concordat with the Papacy, the introduction of the Code Napoleon and the defeat of the Second Coalition. In the ten years after his coronation as Emperor, he defeated in turn the armies of Russia, Austria and Prussia, and filled the thrones of Europe with members of his family. The Russian campaign of 1812, and the Battle of Nations (Leipzig) in 1813 saw the Empire brought low and Napoleon's first abdication in 1814. He escaped from his island prison of Elba in 1815, to begin the 100 days campaign and re-establish the Empire. The Battle of Waterloo in 1815 marked his final defeat and permanent exile to St Helena. The Empire was replaced with the restored Bourbon monarchy, and Louis XVIII became King of France.

Provence, Comte de, Louis Stanislas Xavier (1755-1824) The future Louis XVIII of France (1814-24), Louis was the fourth son of the Dauphin, heir to Louis XV. His eldest surviving brother succeeded his grandfather, to become Louis XVI. Ambitious, the younger Louis was disappointed when his brother had children, who became heir to the throne in place of himself. Against reviving the parlements, he later advocated double representation for the Third Estate. His advice was not normally heeded, and he also fled when Louis and Marie Antoinette tried to escape from France. Unlike them, he was successful, and he joined his brother, Charles, Comte d'Artois, in Brussels. A court in exile was set up, and the behaviour of Provence and Artois was sufficiently galling to the revolutionaries to significantly worsen the position of their brother and sister-in-law. Louis proclaimed himself Regent in 1793, and on the presumed death of Louis XVI's young son, Louis XVII, in June 1795, became Louis XVIII, King-in-exile. For two decades Louis roamed Europe as an exile, travelling from Brunswick to Russia, from Poland to England. He finally came to the throne in March 1814, lost it again during the 100 Days, and regained it in July 1815. As King, Louis accepted the need for a constitution, granted his people a charter of rights, and attempted to preside over a representative parliamentary state.

Robespierre, Maximilien-Françoise-Marie-Isidore (1758-94) The leading Jacobin, Robespierre is best known for his use of the "Terror" as a means of strengthening the revolutionary will of the people. He used the Paris mob to dominate the Convention and bring down the Girondins. Elected to the Assembly in

53 Robespierre.

1789, he had soon become a noted speaker, gaining the Presidency of the Jacobin Club in 1790. As a disciple of Rousseau, he was in favour of universal suffrage, freedom from repression, and public careers open to the talents, whilst condemning autocracy and the oppression of minority groups (such as negro slaves, actors and Jews). After the King's flight to Varennes, he demanded the trial of Louis as a traitor. He was opposed to Brissot's war policy, and when things went badly, was able to put himself forward as the one who had urged caution. The war turned out to be very useful to Robespierre, as it enabled him to justify the Terror as a means of eliminating the enemies of France – by which he meant the possible opponents, past, present and future, of the Jacobin clique. His personal popularity with the people was at its height at this time (1793), and the Committee of Public Safety gave him virtually dictatorial powers from mid-1793. Eventually, the Hébertists, Danton and Camille Desmoulins, fell to the guillotine. Robespierre initiated the cult of the Supreme Being, and this made some suspect him of having delusions. His ruthlessness led to his downfall. No one felt safe, even members of the Committee of Public Safety. The coup of Thermidor ended his power. On his arrest, he attempted suicide, but failed. He was guillotined on the Place de la Révolution.

Rousseau, Jean-Jacques (1717-78) A political philosopher, born in Geneva, whose major treatise, *The Social Contract*, argued that a just society could only be achieved by a government derived from "the will of the people". As Rousseau never clearly explained how the people's will might be discovered, this theory, which was popular among the Jacobins, allowed would-be political leaders to assume that they alone held the key to the popular will and made them intolerant of any disagreement.

Sièyes, Emmanuel Joseph (known as Abbé Sièyes) (1748-1836) A churchman with little vocation, Sièyes became one of the political theorists who inspired the early stages of the revolution. A sympathizer with the poor peasantry, he wrote in 1789 a 20,000-word pamphlet entitled *What is the Third Estate?* Sièyes' answer to this question was: "Everything"; the Third Estate should be acknowledged as the true representative of the people of France and be empowered to create a constitution limiting the powers of the government. Thus Sièyes set in motion the train of events that led from the Tennis Court Oath to the foundation of the National Assembly. Thereafter, however, he became estranged from the growing

54 In this critical cartoon, Sièyes and other Churchmen follow the funeral procession of clergymen who willingly handed over to the state the wealth of the Church. To the artist, this move signified the death of the Church.

violence of the revolution and retired into private life, declaring in old age that his most important activity under the Terror had been to "stay alive". Returning to politics after the coup of Thermidor, he became a Director in 1798, helped Napoleon to seize power, and wrote the first Napoleonic constitution – the Consulate. Exiled in 1814, he returned to France in 1830, under the protection of King Louis Philippe.

Talleyrand, Charles Maurice de (1754-1838) An aristocratic recruit to the Church, worldly and undevout, Talleyrand became Bishop of Autun at the age of thirty-five. An early supporter of the revolution, he piloted the donation of Church property to the state, accepted the Civil Constitution of Clergy and presided over the mass celebrating the first anniversary of the fall of the Bastille. With Louis XVI's execution, however, his aristocratic origins made him increasingly suspect and he emigrated. Returning to France in 1796, Talleyrand proceeded to hold high office under every government until 1834. Having served as Napoleon's Foreign Minister between 1799 and 1808, he corresponded secretly with the Allies and engineered the Bourbon restoration. Deserting the Bourbon cause after 1824, he played a prominent role in the accession of Louis Philippe in 1830. In his memoirs, Talleyrand claimed that his changes of course had never been motivated by self-interest and that he had never deserted a regime until it itself had ceased to govern in the interests of France. Few historians accept this claim without reservations.

Date List

1789

April	Reveillon Riots.
5 May	1st meeting of Estates General.
17 June	Third Estate declares itself the National Assembly.
20 June	Tennis Court Oath.
27 June	King orders nobility and clergy to join Commons.
14 July	Fall of the Bastille.
July-August	"The Great Fear" in the countryside.
4 August	Abolition of feudal rights and privileges.
26 August	Declaration of Rights.
5-6 October	March of women to Versailles and return of King to Paris.
31 October	Establishment of uniform tariff throughout France.
2 November	Nationalization of Church property.
12 December	First issue of Assignats.

1790

21 May	Paris organized into Sections.
19 June	Abolition of nobility.
12 July	Civil Constitution of the Clergy.
14 July	First Fête de la Fédération, celebrating anniversary of fall of Bastille.

1791

2 April	Death of Mirabeau.
16 May	Self-Denying Ordinance – no deputies of National Assembly to be elected as delegates to first Legislative Assembly.
20 June	Flight to Varennes.
17 July	Massacre in Champs de Mars.
27 August	Declaration of Pillnitz.
14 September	King accepts the Constitution.
30 September	Dissolution of National Assembly.
1 October	First meeting of Legislative Assembly.
20 October	Brissot calls for military action to disperse emigrés.

1792

20 April	Declaration of war on Austria.
20 June	First invasion of the Tuileries.
29 June	Lafayette attempts to close Jacobin Club.
22 July	Proclamation of "La Patrie en Danger".
30 July	Marseillais reach Paris.
31 July	Mauconseil Section of Paris repudiates allegiance to monarchy.
3 August	Sections petition for deposition of King.
10 August	Second invasion of Tuileries. Suspension and imprisonment of King.
17 August	Commune forces Assembly to create Extraordinary Tribunal of 17 August.
19 August	Defection of Lafayette. Prussians cross the frontier.
30 August	Assembly attempts to dissolve Commune.
2 September	Fall of fortress of Verdun.
2-6 September	September Massacres.
20 September	Battle of Valmy.
21 September	First session of Convention.
22 September	Beginning of Year I.

YEAR I

24-25 Sept	Girondins attack power of Paris.
10 October	Brissot expelled from Jacobin Club.
19 October	Sections defend power of Paris.
5 November	Robespierre defends Paris and Montagnards.
6 November	Battle of Jemappes – French conquest of Belgium.
19 November	France offers aid to all peoples fighting for their liberty.
20 November	Discovery of "secret cupboard" in Tuileries.

1793

14-17 January	Convention votes to decide fate of King.
21 January	Execution of Louis XVI.
1 February	Declaration of war on Great Britain.
24 February	Levy of 300,000 men decreed.
25 February	Food riots in Paris, of which Jacobins take advantage to increase popularity.
1-7 March	Anti-French revolt in Belgium.
7 March	Declaration of war against Spain.
10 March	Revolutionary Tribunal set up, following rumours of plots against Convention.
16 March	Outbreak of revolt in Vendée.
18 March	Battle of Neerwinden. Dumouriez evacuates Brussels.
21 March	Creation of local Revolutionary Committees.
5 April	Defection of Dumouriez.
6 April	Creation of Committee of Public Safety.
13 April	Impeachment of Marat.
15 April	Sections demand a purge of the Convention.
4 May	First "Maximum" on food prices declared.
10 May	Convention moves to Tuileries.
20 May	Commission of Twelve appointed to investigate plots against Convention.
30 May	Conservative coup d'état in Lyons.
2 June	Revolution of 2nd June. Convention purged by Section and Montagnards. Brissot arrested. His supporters flee to Bordeaux and Caen.
9 June	Vendéans take Saumur.
24 June	Convention accepts constitution of 1793.
10 July	Danton ceases to be a member of Committee of Public Safety.
11 July	Murder of Marat.
26 July	Decree makes hoarding a capital crime.
27 July	Robespierre enters Committee of Public Safety.
28 July	18 Girondin deputies outlawed.
23 August	Declaration of Levée en masse.
27 August	Surrender of Toulon to British.
5 September	Hébertist rising in Paris. Terror becomes order of the day.
17 September	Law of Suspects issued.

YEAR II

22 September	Year II begins.
29 September	General "Maximum" in restraint of prices and wages.
3 September	Impeachment of Brissot and 44 other deputies.
9 September	Recapture of Lyons.

10 September	Decree sanctioning "Revolutionary Government" for duration of the war.	15 March	Conquest of Papal States. Establishment of Roman Republic.
16 September	Battle of Wattignies. Execution of Marie Antoinette.	21 July	French victory at Battle of the Pyramids – first stage in attempt to defeat Britain by severing her trade links. French entry into Cairo.
17 September	Vendéans defeated at Cholet.		
24-31 October	Trial and execution of Girondins.		
10 November	Festival of Reason in Notre Dame.	1 August	French defeat at Battle of the Nile (Aboukir Bay).
22 November	Closure of churches in Paris.		
November	Massacres at Nantes.		
4 December	Law of Revolutionary Government (Law of 14 Frimaire). Massacres at Lyons.		

1799

13 October	Napoleon lands in France.
9-10 November	Coup d'état of 18 Brumaire. Napoleon Bonaparte becomes First Consul.

23 December	Defeat of Vendéans at Savenay.

1794

26 February	Laws of Ventose.
14 March	Arrest of Hébertists.
24 March	Execution of Hébertists.
30 March	Arrest of Danton.
5 April	Execution of Dantonists.
23 May	Presumed attempted assassination of Robespierre by Admiral.
24 May	Presumed attempted assassination of Robespierre by Cecile Renault.
1 June	British naval victory off Brest – "The Glorious 1st of June".
7 June	Festival of the Supreme Being in Paris.
10 June	Law of Prairial, severely restricting rights of accused before Revolutionary Tribunal.
26 June	Battle of Fleurus. French reconquest of Belgium.
27 July	Proscription of Robespierre, Saint-Just and Couthon in plot of Thermidor.
28 July	Execution of Robespierre and others.
30-31-July	Reorganization of Committee of Public Safety.
17 November	Closure of Jacobin Club.
16 December	Execution of Carrier.
24 December	Abolition of Maximum.

1795

5 April	Peace of Basle with Prussians.
8 June	Death of Louis XVII. Comte de Provence declares himself Louis XVIII.
21 July	Hoche defeats emigré forces at Quiberon.
5 October	Revolt of 13 Vendémiaire.
26 October	Dissolution of Convention. Rule of Directory begins.

1796

17 March	Napoleon Bonaparte receives command of Army in Italy.
March	Elections to new Legislature produce a royalist majority.
11 May	Defeat of Babeuf conspiracy.

1797

	Conquest of Italy and creation of "republics" dependent on France.
October	Peace of Campo Formio with Austria. Belgium, North Italy and Rhineland brought under French control.
4 September	Coup of Fruchtidor. With help of units of the army, led by Napoleon's lieutenant, Augureau, the legislature is purged of its royalist element.

1798

22 March	Conquest of Switzerland. Helvetian Republic announced.

THE REVOLUTIONARY CALENDAR

To symbolize that the revolution meant a complete break with a superstitious and religious past, the traditional (Gregorian) calendar was abandoned in favour of a "revolutionary" calendar, in which the names of the months were derived from events in the natural world. The New Year began on 22 September, the anniversary of the abolition of royalty, and September 1792 – September 1793 became Year I of the Republic. It is from the names of the revolutionary months that the names given by history to the dramatic events of the revolution are derived: for example, Coup of Thermidor (July 1794). Here is a list of the revolutionary months and their equivalents in the Gregorian calendar.

Revolutionary Months		*Gregorian Calendar*
Vendémiaire	1-30 month of vintage	22 September – 21 October
Brumaire	1-30 month of fog	22 October – 20 November
Frimaire	1-30 month of frost	21 November – 20 December
Nivose	1-30 month of snow	21 December – 19 January
Pluviose	1-30 month of rain	20 January – 18 February
Ventose	1-30 month of wind	19 February – 20 March
Germinal	1-30 month of budding	21 March – 19 April
Floreal	1-30 month of flowers	20 April – 19 May
Prairial	1-30 month of meadows	20 May – 18 June
Messidor	1-30 month of harvest	19 June – 18 July
Thermidor	1-30 month of heat	19 July – 17 August
Fruchtidor	1-30 month of fruit	18 August – 16 September

The five spare days, 17-21 September, were named, collectively, *sans-culottides*. The seven-day week gave way to one of ten days, called a "decade", Sundays and saints' days being replaced by a public holiday every tenth day. Each of the three hundred and sixty days was named after a natural object in the animal or vegetable kingdom. The 3 Brumaire, for example, was the Day of Pears. The five sans-culottides were called after Republican virtues.

GLOSSARY

Ancien Régime A term applied to the political and social system of France before 1789. Among its most prominent and criticized features were absolute monarchical rule and a rigid class structure, in which class was determined purely by birth and could not be affected by wealth or education. Duties and privileges were strictly assigned to each class. Nobles, for example, were exempt from most forms of taxation and had exclusive right to officer status in the army, but they were forbidden to earn a living by trade or by the practice of a profession.

Assembly of Notables Meeting of the nobility of France, summoned by Louis XVI in February 1787 to deal with the bankruptcy of the government. Calonne, Controller-General of Finances, proposed to introduce a general land-tax, from which there would be no exemptions; such a tax would be unenforceable if the consent of the nobility were not first obtained. The Assembly was dissolved as a failure in May 1787.

Bastille Day Decreed by the Assembly in 1790 as an annual fete to be held on 14 July, the anniversary of the fall of the Bastille. Bastille Day was the first of the spectacular Republican pageants that were intended to replace the banned religious festivals, and it is the only one still celebrated as a public holiday in France.

Civil Constitution of Clergy Law of July 1790, which aimed to bring the Church under state control. Bishops and priests were to be elected by the laity, religious orders were dissolved, and all clergy required to swear an oath of loyalty to the constitution. Condemned by the Vatican in March 1791, less than half the clergy accepted the changes, and many were thus driven into exile and outright opposition to the revolution.

Committee of General Security (Police Committee) Committee of the Convention, elected by the same system as the Committee of Public Safety, responsible for police work, including the employment of spies and the making of arrests.

Committee of Public Safety Established by the National Convention in April 1793, to have overall supervision of the activities of the Convention and the government ministries. Elected from the members of the Convention for a month at a time, it became the most powerful body in France, dominating the Convention in whose name it was supposed to act. From July 1793 to July 1794 the twelve-man committee was dominated by the personality of Maximilien Robespierre.

Commune of Paris Municipal government of Paris, established in 1789, to replace the old City Council. Elected by popular vote, the Commune tended to be a radical body, of whose views the government of the day was forced to take note.

Counter-revolution Attempt by those ousted from power by a revolution to return to the old order.

Estates General (States General) Traditional Assembly designed to represent the three classes of French society. It was summonable only by the will of the monarch, and had not met for 175 years when Louis XVI called it in May 1789, in an attempt to find a way out of the financial impasse (see Assembly of Notables).

Feudal system Traditional system of seigneurial rights that went with the ownership of land. Among these rights were the peasant's obligation to use his landlord's mill or wine-press, the right of a landowner to feed his pigeons and rabbits on the peasant's crops, and his right to levy tolls on local roads and rivers. The feudal system was partially abolished by the Assembly in August 1789 and completely ended by the Convention in 1793.

"The Great Fear" Spontaneous outburst of violence in rural areas of France in the summer of 1789, triggered off by rumours that bands of "brigands" were roaming the countryside and threatening the peasants' livelihood. The violence was aimed at the destruction of feudal records rather than at the persons of the landowners, and was one of the factors that persuaded the Assembly to abolish some of the feudal dues in August 1789.

Girondins Group of deputies in the Assembly and National Convention 1791-93. Many (although not all) of them came from the Gironde district around Bordeaux. Until the end of 1792 they were among the most radical groups in France, favouring the foundation of a republic and the war against foreign monarchies, and, with reservations, the execution of the King. In 1793 the Girondins were out-manoeuvred by the Jacobins, who had the support of the Parisian masses, and were outlawed in June of that year. Some fled to Caen and Bordeaux, where unsuccessful revolts against the Jacobins were staged. In October 1793 all the prominent Girondist leaders were executed. They are sometimes known as "Brissotins", after one of their leaders, Brissot.

Hébertists Followers of Hébert, editor of the popular newspaper, *Père Duchesne*. Influential in the Paris Commune between 1792 and 1794, they advocated government policies tailored in the interests of the working classes of Paris and were powerful enough to force important governmental changes in July 1793. Hébertists were primarily responsible for the imposition of the Maximum. Their power was broken when the Committee of Public Safety arrested and executed Hébert and other leaders in March 1794.

Jacobins Group of radical deputies in the Convention, who drew much of their influence from their popularity with the Paris sections. By June 1793 they dominated the Committee of Public Safety, and for a year, 1793-94,

55 The Jacobin as he saw himself – the guardian of liberty. Note that he is wearing trousers rather than knee-breeches; from this stemmed the popular name "sans-culottes".

imposed their will on the rest of France, through the system known as the "Terror". Their dictatorship was broken by the coup of Thermidor and the execution of their leaders. The name derives from the meeting place of the Jacobin Club at the former Dominican monastery in the Rue St Honoré; Dominican monks had long been nicknamed "Jacobins", because their original Paris home was the Monastery of St Jacques. Also known as the "Mountain" (*see below*).

Law of Prairial Law of 10 June 1794 which denied the right of defence to those accused before the Revolutionary Tribunal, and allowed no verdict but acquittal or death.

Law of Suspects Law of 17 September 1793 which provided a codified definition of all types of person who were to be considered as "counter-revolutionaries". The categories of "suspects" were very wide, so that almost anyone could be included (*see page 43*).

Lettres de Cachet Device of the Ancien Régime whereby the monarch could override the normal course of justice and issue a warrant arresting and incarcerating at his pleasure. At the instigation of their families, both Mirabeau and Saint-Just were imprisoned for a while under this system.

Livre In 1789 in Anjou an ordinary farm labourer would earn one livre for between one and two days work. This would buy about 3 pounds of butter, or two capons, or two geese, or a pound of wax, or almost a bushel of rye. The rent for an average farm would be about 500 livres per year, and a typical farmer would own household goods worth about 200 livres. (Charles Tilly, *The Vendée*, Wiley. New York. 1967)

Maximum A series of laws (the most important was that of 29 September 1793) which were enacted under pressure from the Paris sections. Maximum prices were set for staple commodities such as meat, bread, wine, candles and tobacco, and the minimum level of wages was laid down. This attempt to curb the inflation which had severely affected the poorer city wage-earners since 1789 is generally considered to have done more harm than good, for peasants hoarded their produce in the hope of obtaining higher prices in the future, and severe shortages of all commodities occurred in the winter and spring of 1793-94.

Mountain (Montagnards) Popular name for the Jacobins. It came from the position that Jacobin deputies occupied in the Convention, where they sat on the seats high up at the back of the hall.

National Assembly Created on 17 June 1789, when the Third Estate of the Estates General declared itself to be the body most truly representative of the nation. This development became permanent when the King was forced to return to Paris from Versailles in October 1789 and became, in effect, a prisoner of the Assembly and the people of Paris. The Assembly called itself the Constituent Assembly from 9 July 1789 onwards.

National Convention Replaced the Assembly as the ruling body of France when the monarchy was suspended in August 1792. Elected by universal suffrage, the Convention ruled France until the establishment of the Directory, in October 1795, and was dominated in turn by the Girondins and the Jacobins. One of its first activities was the declaration of the Republic in September 1792. From mid-1793 to mid-1794 the Convention played a secondary role to the Committee of Public Safety.

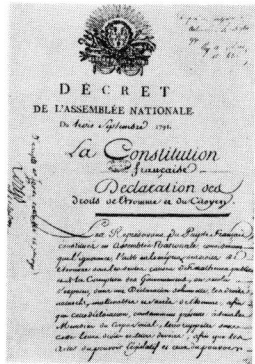

56 The drafting of the Constitution of 1791, embodying the Rights of Man, was one of the most important tasks of the National Assembly. It bears Louis XVI's signature.

National Guard A company of volunteers formed in Paris in July 1789, to defend the gains of the revolution against real or imaginary aristocratic plots and to protect property against pillage. Its first commander was Lafayette. As the revolution proceeded, the National Guard became increasingly identified with the defence of middle-class moderation against sans-culottes demands for complete political and social change. For example, on 16 July 1791 a popular demonstration was held on the Champs de Mars to draw up a petition calling for the King's abdication. When two suspected spies were lynched by the crowd, the National Guard intervened to restore order. In the ensuing panic, fifty members of the crowd and two National Guardsmen were killed.

Parlements Six regional assemblies, the most important of which was the parlement of Paris, functioned as the highest courts in the land, with the right to register and authorise the decrees issued by the King and council. Composed of distinguished lawyers, in the period before 1789 the parlements obstructed the policies of Louis XV and Louis XVI and posed as the champions of the people against royal absolutism. In fact, they were concerned almost exclusively with the protection of the interests of the wealthy middle class; and, by obstructing reform of the financial system (which might hurt the pockets of the middle class), they contributed to the causes of the revolution.

Representatives on Mission Members of the Convention who were dispatched to supervise the conduct of revolutionary committees and the Republican Army in the provinces. In an era of slow communications, it was the only way to ensure a measure of uniformity in the policies pursued by revolutionaries in different parts of France; and the only way that the government could keep itself informed of public opinion outside Paris. Representatives had wide-ranging powers; for example, they could dismiss and appoint army commanders. Representatives were supposed to write once a week to the Convention (after July 1793 the Committee of Public Safety usurped this function) and obey Paris in all matters. However, in practice, the system proved difficult to control and Representatives often behaved in a tyrannical and idiosyncratic way.

Revolutionary Tribunal Established in Paris in February 1793, as an extraordinary court to judge those suspected of disloyalty to the revolution. Its procedures became increasingly summary (*see* Law of Prairial), although the sum of its victims was always far outnumbered by those executed, legally and illegally, in the provinces.

Sans-culottes Blanket term given to the radicals of Paris, most of whom were drawn from the class of artisans and small shopkeepers. They were never a homogeneous group and included a number of different factions, among which were the Hébertists and the Enragés. Between 1791 and 1794 threats of violence towards the Assembly and the Convention forced these bodies to adopt ever more extreme policies, and the Jacobins rose to power with the backing of the sans-culottes. Their power was severely weakened by the execution of Hébert and other leaders in March 1794. The name derives from the artisan custom of wearing long trousers instead of aristocratic knee-breeches.

Sections (of Paris) 48 sub-divisions of the Paris Commune, responsible for the policing of each locality.

Swiss Guard Part of the French tradition of raising regiments of foreign mercenaries for royal service, of which the French Foreign Legion is a modern example. The Swiss had the reputation of being Europe's most efficient and reliable mercenaries (provided they were regularly paid), and since the sixteenth century they had provided elite personal bodyguards for the Kings of France and the Popes.

Thermidor Successful plot of 27-28 July 1794, by disaffected Jacobins, which resulted in the deposition of Robespierre and his closest associates. Among the conspirators were Fouché, Barras and Carrier.

Third Estate All Frenchmen who did not belong to the First Estate (hereditary nobility) or Second Estate (clergy) belonged to this class (*see* Ancien Régime).

57 This cartoonist believed that the downfall of Robespierre and Saint-Just was richly deserved. Under the protecting eye and ear of Justice, flies the avenging spirit of Thermidor, carrying a basket containing the heads of the members of the Revolutionary Tribunal. Two accompanying furies bear the heads of Robespierre, Couthon, Saint-Just and Carrier. Note the fashionable classical style with figures from Greek mythology.

Consequently, it contained the bulk of the French population, ranging from the wealthiest member of the middle class to the poorest peasant.

Tuileries Paris Palace of the Kings of France, deserted since Louis XIV's removal of the court to Versailles in 1671. When Louis XVI was forcibly brought back to the Tuileries in October 1789, the dictatorship of Paris over the course of the revolution, which lasted until 1795, began (*see* Vendémiaire). In August 1792 the invasion of the Tuileries by the Paris mob resulted in the suspension of the monarchy and the imprisonment of the King.

Vendée Region of western France between the port of La Rochelle and the mouth of the Loire. The revolt which broke out there in March 1793 was partly royalist and religious in inspiration, and partly the result of the introduction of conscription and requisitioning in an area traditionally suspicious of government from Paris. The revolt was suppressed in the autumn of 1793 (*see* Carrier, page 18) but smouldered on until complete pacification was achieved by Napoleon's expedition of 1800.

58 A Vendéan rebel asks the Virgin Mary to bless his struggle against the godless Republic.

Vendémiaire Unsuccessful uprising in Paris by royalists who had infiltrated the Paris sections, September 1795. Its suppression by the army, under the command of Barras and Napoleon Bonaparte, broke the power of Paris over the course of the revolution.

Books For Further Reading

Introductory Books
D. Johnson, *The French Revolution* (Wayland, 1970)
M. Rosenthal, *The French Revolution* (Longmans, *Then and There* series, 1965)

More Advanced Books
W. Doyle, *The Origins of the French Revolution* (O.U.P., 1980)
N. Hampson, *A Social History of the French Revolution* (Routledge and Kegan Paul, *Studies in Social History*, 1963)
J. Roberts, *The French Revolution* (O.U.P., 1978)
M.J. Sydenham, *The French Revolution* (Batsford/Methuen, 1965)

Collections of Reminiscences
G. Pernoud and S. Flaissier, *The French Revolution* (Secker and Warburg, 1960)

Collections of Documents
J. Hardman, *The French Revolution. The Fall of the Ancien Regime to the Thermidorian Reaction 1789-1795* (Edward Arnold, 1981)
J.M. Thompson, *The French Revolution* (Blackwell, 1943)
D.G. Wright, *Revolution and Terror in France 1789-1795* (Longmans, 1974)

General Background
M.E. Barlow, *The Foundations of Modern Europe 1789-1871* (Bell, 1968)
R.F. Leslie, *The Age of Transformation* (Blandford, 1964)
G. Rude, *Revolutionary Europe 1783-1815* (1964)

Audio-Visual Aids
The French Revolution, Educational Audio Visual Ltd, London (sound filmstrip plus teacher's notes)

Index

The figures in **bold type** refer to pages on which illustrations appear.

Aiguillon, Duc d' 28
America, United States of:
 influence on the French revolution 5, 7, 63
 Chateaubriand in 34
aristocracy in France:
 as a cause of revolution 6f, 29f, **29**
 fate during revolution 28, 42, **50**
 liberal wing of 10, 13, 28, 30, 37-8, 42
Army, Prussian 23, 34f
Army, Republican:
 in Italy 55, 58f
 of the North 18
 of the Rhine 18, 52
 promotion in 11, 23ff, 54f
 recruitment for 22, **22**
 success of 23f
army, royalist 11
Artois, Duc d' 7, 34f, 61
Assembly of Notables 7, 68
Austria, opposition to French Revolution 28f, 50f

Barère, Bertrand 46, 61
Barras, Vicomte Paul de 55, 57, 61, **61**
Bastille 10, 11ff, **12, 13**, 68
Batz, Baron Jean de 35ff
Beauharnais:
 Alexandre de 53, 63
 Josephine de 29, 53, 63
Bernadotte, Marshal 11, 59f, **59**
Bonaparte, Napoleon:
 and Army of Italy 55
 and the Directory 55
 and Fouché 55, 57f
 and Massena 59
 and Vendémiaire 55
 as First Consul 35
 short biography of **54**, 64
Bordeaux **5**, 28, 31f
Brissot, Jacques Pierre 29, 61f
Britain, opposition to French revolution 28, **41, 61**
Brunswick Manifesto 16

Caen 28, 38
Calonne 14
Carlyle, Thomas 11
Carmes Prison 52f
Carnot, Lazare 11, 17, 41, 54, 55, 62
Carrier, Jean-Baptiste **5**, 18ff, **19**, 46
Chabot 36, **37**
Champs de Mars, massacre of 63, 69
Chartres, Duc d' 44f, 62
Chateaubriand, François René de 33ff, **33**, 55
Chenier, André 27
clergy:
 civil constitution of 28, 68
 reaction to revolution 28, **65**
Cobb, Richard, historian 27, 60
Cobban, Alfred, historian 19
Cochon de Lapperant 60
Collot d'Herbois, Jean-Marie 10, 17, 56f, **56**, 62
Committee of General Security 26, 27, 36
Committee of Public Safety:
 activities of 20f, 46f, 53

membership of 17, 68
origins of 10, 17
Corday, Charlotte 37ff, **39**
Couthon, Georges 18, 62

Danton, Georges 17f, 42, 62
David, Jacques-Louis:
    life of 24ff, **25**
    examples of his art **25**, **34**
de Launay **34**, 42
Desmoulins, Camille 16f, 63
Directory 26, 55, 57
Dumouriez, General 17, 18, 28

Elliot, Grace:
    life of 51ff
    on Duke of Orleans 44ff
emigrés:
    army of 34f, 42
    composition of 28f
    experiences of 35
    Madame de la Tour du Pin on 30
Estates General 7ff, **8**, 14, 68

festivals:
    of Reason **26**
    of the Supreme Being 25
Fouché, Joseph 5, 18, 46, 55ff, **56**
Fouquier-Tinville, Antoine-Quentin **47**, 48, 54, 63

Girondins 17, 28, 38f, 42, 68
Guenot, Nicholas 11, 26f

Hébert, Jacques 10f, 42, 68
Hérault de Séchelles, Marie-Jean 18, 20, 63
Hesdin, Raoul 40f
Hoche, Lazare 52f, 63
Humbert, Jean-Baptiste 11ff

Invalides, Les 11f, 21

Jacobins 16f, **17**, **19**, 38f, 40, 68f, **69**
Jefferson, Thomas 5ff
Jemappes, Battle of **5**, **23**

Lafayette, Adrienne 48ff
Lafayette, Marquis de 28, 48ff passim, **49**, 63f
Lafayette, Virginie 48ff passim
Louis XVI:
    and the revolution 10, 15
    as King 6ff

execution of 17, 28, **31**, 45
Lyons 5, 28, 43, 56f, **56**

Marat, Jean Paul 16f:
    assassination of 24f, 38f, **39**
    short biography of 64
Marie Antoinette 6f, **25**, 29, 36, 43, 64
Massena, André 11, 58f, **59**
Maximum, Law of 40, 69
Mirabeau, Comte de:
    life of 13ff
    Morris on 8
    on causes of the revolution 7
    on Louis Philippe 44
Morris, Gouverneur 6ff, 15
Mountain (Montagne) 16, 26, 39, 69
    (*see also* Jacobins)

Nantes 5, **16**, 18ff, 56
National Assembly 14f, 69
National Convention 16, 45, 69
National Guard 21f, 69
Necker, Jacques 14
Neerwinden, battle of 5, 28
Noailles, Vicomte de 28, 30

Orleans, Louis Philippe, Duke of 42, **43**:
    life of 43ff
    Young on 8

Palmer, R. R., historian 21
Paris 5, **9**:
    as pace-setter of revolution 5, 10, 28, 55, 70
    commune of 31, 68
    life in 40ff
    Parlement of 6f, 69f
    sections of 70
peasantry, French:
    under Ancien Régime 6
    role in revolution 10
Pillnitz, Declaration of 29
Prairial, Law of 48, 69
Provence, Duc de 37, 64

rationing:
    in army 23
    in Bordeaux 32
    in Paris 40
Renault, Cecile 46ff
Representatives on Mission:
    activities of 23, 70
    Carrier as 18ff

Fouché as 56f
Saint-Just as 18
Revolutionary Tribunal 48, 70
Robespierre, Augustin 55
Robespierre, Charlotte 55f
Robespierre, Maximilien 16, **64**:
    and Fouché 55ff
    as dictator 41
    fall of 18, 41, 42, 53
    (*see also* Thermidor, coup of)
    political philosophy of 10, 42f
    short biography of 64f
Rousseau, Jean-Jacques **15**:
    influence on American revolution of 5
    influence on French revolution of 10, 65
Roux, Jacques 42f

Saint-Just, Louis Antoine de:
    and General Hoche 52, 63
    Hesdin on 41
    life of 16ff
    political philosophy of 10, 16ff
sans-culottes 10, 40, **69**, 70
September Massacres 10, 42
Sièyes, Abbé 8, 65
St Antoine, Faubourg of 10, 44
Suspects, Law of 43, 49, 69
Swiss Guard 9, 12f, 51, 70

Talleyrand, Charles Maurice de 57
Tennis Court, Oath of **8**, 9, 24, 26
Terror, the 18, 40f, **52**, **53**
Thermidor, coup of 18, 21, 26, 54, 57, 70
Thiebault, Paul de 21ff
Tour du Pin, Comtesse de la:
    life of 29ff
    on Duke of Orleans 44
Tuileries, Palace of 15f, 51, 70

Valmy, Battle of **5**, 23, 34f
Vendée 5, 10, 17, 18ff, 28, 43, **70**
Vendémiaire, rising of 37, 55
Versailles 29:
    as meeting place of Estates General 8f, **8**
    march of women to 44, **45**
Voltaire 5, **15**

Washington, George 7, 34
White Terror 28, 54, 57

Young, Arthur 5ff